The Belvedere Academy

This book is due for return on or before that last date shown below.

SELF PORTRAITS
of the THE WORLD'S
GREATEST
PAINTERS

MILLY CHILDERS (active 1888–1920), 1889
(City Art Gallery, Leeds Museums and Galleries, England)
(*See page 90*)

SELF PORTRAITS
of the THE WORLD'S
GREATEST
PAINTERS

ELIZABETH DRURY

PARKGATE
BOOKS

THE BRIDGEMAN ART LIBRARY

Research at the Bridgeman Art Library was by Ed Whitley.
All the images featured in this book were supplied by The Bridgeman Art Library. A commercial fine art photograpgic library consisting
of over 100,000 images, the archive ranges from prehistoric cave paintings to the work of contemporary artists. There is an extensive selection
of sculpture, ceramics, furniture, ancient artefacts and general objets d'art.
The Bridgeman Art Library represents over 800 collections from around the world and is expanding by 300 new images weekly.
A CD-ROM of the archive is now available and images can be viewed and ordered at our
website — Website: http//www.bridgeman.co.uk.
For further information contact one of our three offices:
The Bridgeman Art Library
17–19 Garway Road

London W2 4PH

Tel: +44 (0)207 727 4065
Fax: +44 (0)207 792 8509
E-mail: info@bridgeman.co.uk
65 East 93rd Street
New York

NY 10128

Tel: +1 212 828 1238
Fax: +1 212 828 1255
E-mail: info@bridgemanart.com
31 rue Etienne Marcel
75001 Paris

Tel: +33 (0)1 53 40 70 60
Fax: +33 (0)1 53 40 82 20
E-mail: paris@bridgeman.co.uk

TEXT RESEARCH

Suzanne Bailey, Dorian Church, Emily Cole, Susanna Wright

First published in 1999 by
PRC Publishing Ltd,
Kiln House, 210 New Kings Road, London SW6 4NZ

This edition published in 1999 by
Parkgate Books
London House
Great Eastern Wharf
Parkgate Road
London
SW11 4NQ

British Library Cataloguing in Publication Data:
A catalogue record for this book is available from the British Library.

ISBN 1 902616 54 5

Printed and bound in China

CONTENTS

INTRODUCTION

A self-portrait is a form of autobiography. It is the record of an artist's perception of himself — or herself — and of how he wishes to be remembered. In due course it may become the artist's epitaph. This seems to be true in the case of Rembrandt and Van Gogh, two painters who left a series of portraits of themselves that serve as memorials to them, as men and in particular as artists.

The portrait may have been made for some personal reason, in the interests of self-knowledge or as practice for painting portraits of others and figure compositions, the artist using himself as the model; or perhaps with other people in mind — a patron or a collector — attracting attention to himself and his artistic ability. He may even have been invited or requested to provide a portrait.

As the creator as well as the subject of the picture, he is able to communicate exactly what he feels about himself. Staring at his face in the mirror or searching his mind and memory, the artist gives a visual account of himself. He can present himself as a person of standing, full of confidence about his place in the world and his talent. He can even produce an enhanced or idealized impression, persuading the viewer that he is better looking or more important and successful than he really is; that it would be a pleasure to sit to him for a portrait and the result likely to please. He can do the opposite, contemplating his appearance and lot in life with dismay, and sharing his feelings of anxiety and bewilderment with anyone who looks at the picture.

Autobiographies are written for the amusement or interest of their subject in the same way; or else for the record — perhaps to put the record straight. There may be an element of self-promotion here too. If the account is published there will be readers, taking the place of the viewers of a work of art. Setting down in writing the facts, or his version of the

Self-portrait by Luis Egidio Meléndez (1716–80), 1746. The image of the Spanish artist expresses self-esteem, and his skill as a painter of the portrait no doubt impressed potential patrons. (Musée du Louvre, Paris, France)

facts, the author is able to describe what he did, where he went, the people he met and what he thought of them, his views and opinions. He, too, can exaggerate or alter the facts, choosing to omit details he does not wish to be remembered. He describes his life and the world around him from his own perspective.

It might seem that a written self-portrait is more revealing of the subject than a painted self-portrait; or at least that the 'picture' that is put across is clearer. This may be true, but while looking through the illustrations in this book it is worth searching for information and making some deductions. The process and conclusions will, it is hoped, add to the appreciation of the images and generate curiosity about the artists and their lives.

The most obvious and important point is that artists portray themselves in the manner in which they were working at the time, whatever their subject-matter. The technique and palette, and all the other components of their manner of painting, drawing or printmaking, often show the influence of their contemporaries and conform in some degree to the conventions and fashions of the age. They reflect the circle in which the artist moved. Even if his or her face is not immediately recognizable (from other portraits or, since the mid-nineteenth century, from photographs), it is often possible to say that the artist was living in, or came from, a particular country — at a particular time.

The setting and background, the costume and the way of dressing the hair provide clues, even though some of the details might have a symbolic rather than an actual relevance to the person depicted. Most instructive of all is whether an attempt seems to have been made to produce a truthful likeness — a mirror-image of the artist/model — or a representative image, with only a few indications of the physical traits of the sitter, or a

Self-portrait by Rosalba Carriera (1675-1757), 1709. Autobiographical details include the artist's style of dress and the fact that she is working on a portrait in pastels. (Galleria degli Uffizi, Florence, Italy)

Detail from The Procession of the Magi by Benozzo Gozzoli (1420–97), 1459. The painter's self-portrait as a figure in the crowd is indicated by the words 'OP. (Palazzo Medici-Riccardi, Florence, Italy)

statement about his temperament and character rather than a study of his physiognomy. All these factors are revealing of the time and circumstances in which the image was created, and thus of the creator.

Self-portraits in Renaissance Narrative Paintings

Benozzo Gozzoli's portrait of himself in the procession of the *Three Magi* — a face in the crowd — is one of the earliest self-portraits to be included in this book. It dates from the mid-fifteenth century.

By representing himself in the scene Gozzoli was, in effect, putting his signature to the work. In the Middle Ages manuscripts would sometimes include the figure of the creator of the illuminations, and craftsmen would claim their part in the decoration of a cathedral façade with a self-likeness in stone. In the fresco in the Palazzo Medici-Riccardi, Gozzoli goes a step further by identifying himself in the gold lettering on his red cap.

Giorgio Vasari, in his *Lives of the Most Excellent Painters, Sculptors and Architects*, first published in 1550, commented on the lifelike quality of the figures in Giotto's paintings. It was Giotto, he said, who introduced 'the custom of accurately drawing living persons from Nature'. Real people were Giotto's models for the figures in his narrative paintings in Florence, Padua and Assisi.

Apart from Gozzoli's own, other faces in the throng were almost certainly modelled on his contemporaries in Renaissance Florence. Because the men can no longer be named, the images cannot be described as portraits, but there is little doubt that at the time the topical interest of the painting — recognition of the artist's models — would have aroused as much interest as the ostensible subject-matter.

Independent, autonomous, portraits do not exist from this period. Even men of high birth and position, such as members of the Medici family, were only portrayed as witnesses to, or participants in, a religious scene, or else as the donor, who commissioned and paid for the work. Botticelli's panel painting of *The Adoration of the Magi* is another that includes figures identified as members of the Medici family — and one that is thought to have been modelled on the artist himself.

Already, in the self-likenesses of these two fifteenth-century painters, a characteristic of much self-portraiture throughout the ages is apparent: the eye-contact between the model (the artist himself) and the person viewing the picture. In many of the images reproduced in this book the sitters gaze steadily out of the picture, the look in their eyes inviting the onlooker to appraise the person portrayed. This is, of course, because in many self-portraits the artist is copying — to a greater or lesser degree of exactitude, perhaps relative to his skill — what he sees when he looks at his own reflection in a mirror.

Mirror-glass and the Mirror-image

Mirrors, in the fifteenth century, were plates of polished metal or else made of convex glass. The latter came principally from Nuremberg, made

Detail from The Adoration of the Magi by Sandro Botticelli (1444/5–1510), early 1470s. he panel painting as a witness to the scene, his gaze directed out of the picture. (Galleria degli Uffizi, Florence, Italy)

by a process in which the molten metallic mixture was blown into a globe and the globe cut in half when it had cooled. The glass was circular in section, the rounded surface reflecting a distorted image that magnified objects close to its surface.

Jan van Eyck included a convex glass in his painting celebrating the marriage of Giovanni Arnolfini to his wife Jeanne. Occupying a place in the centre of the composition, it reflects the backs of the couple, and the figure of Van Eyck himself as the painter of the picture. The illusion is created that Van Eyck is both in and outside the picture.

While mirrors formed part of the furnishings of a domestic interior, in Italy as well as northern Europe, they were also to be found in painters' studios. In 1435, Leon Battista Alberti, author of a treatise on painting, recommended that the artist should use the reflection from a mirror to look for imperfections in his work: 'it is remarkable how every defect in a picture appears more unsightly in a mirror. So the things that are taken from nature should be amended with the advice of the mirror'. Already, the subject, in a mirror-image, was converted into two dimensions, as it would be in the work of art. Leonardo is known to have made use of a glass to perfect his imitations of nature. 'The mirror, above all' he wrote, 'the mirror is our teacher'.

At the beginning of the sixteenth century Antonio and Domenico Gallo, glassmakers of Murano, developed a technique in which a bubble of blown glass was cut down the middle and spread out flat. Once flattened, the glass was cut into small panes, and to create a mirror a metal-leaf

Arnolfini and his Wife by Jan van Eyck (c. 1390–1441), 1434.
The figure of the man dressed in blue reflected in the convex mirror is believed to be a self-portrait of the Netherlandish painter.
(National Gallery, London, England)

backing was applied using mercury. Ripples in the glass produced an imperfect reflection. Venice had a monopoly on the commercial manufacture of mirrors, and in the paintings of the Venetians Titian and Tintoretto we see Venus and Susanna looking at their own reflections in a 'looking-glass'.

The Artist Portrayed

In 1484, Albrecht Dürer, then a boy of thirteen or fourteen, made a fine silverpoint drawing of himself and inscribed it, 'This I drew, using a mirror'. The German artist later made several painted likenesses of himself, for which he must have scrutinized the particulars of his own face in a mirror. Dürer is considered to have been among the first to make portraiture part of his artistic repertoire and to paint autonomous self-portraits.

While taking on important commissions on religious subjects, he worked on others of his own choosing, particularly in the medium of engraving. Intrigued by the studies of perspective and proportion that were being engaged in by the Italians, Dürer made a journey on his own account across the Alps to Venice. He was a man of initiative, independence and invention. He was fêted in the Netherlands as the leader in his profession and a figure of importance. His reputation spread far and wide.

In Dürer's lifetime — he died in 1528 — the standing of a painter grew from that of a simple craftsmen, living by manual labour, to a man of

Self-portrait with Gloves by Albrecht Dürer (1471–1528), 1493. The German artist was among the first in Western art to paint independent self-portraits. (Musée du Louvre, Paris, France)

genius, who possessed a vocation and was recognized for his unique talent. He had a new status in society. There was, too, a general and new emphasis on self-awareness. Men saw themselves as independent beings in charge of their own destiny. They wished to be regarded — and remembered — not simply for their rank or position but as individuals, distinct from their contemporaries and their predecessors.

There was no better way of achieving this than in paintings in which a physical resemblance to them was created, from which their features would be recognized and recorded for posterity. Dürer defined preserving 'the likenesses of men after their death' as one of the purposes of the art of painting. Artists now felt that they deserved recognition — and a stake in immortality — and with the popularity of portrait-painting came the rise of the artist's portrait of himself.

In the early sixteenth century in Italy painters, as well as consorting with men of learning, became the courtiers of princes and popes. Titian's fame spread throughout Europe, and he was appointed court painter to the emperor Charles V, who in 1548, summoned him to Augsburg. Raphael and Michelangelo were called to Rome by Pope Julius II. Titian and Raphael both painted self-portraits, and Raphael even had the temerity to include his likeness in the company of the philosophers in his fresco *The School of Athens* in the Vatican.

Parmigianino, in an attempt to secure the patronage of Pope Clement VII, took with him to Rome one of the most ingenious independent self-portraits of the High Renaissance. He commissioned a turner to make him a wooden ball, which, when it had been cut in half, would replicate the size and shape of a convex 'barber's mirror'. On the curved surface of this he copied in paint 'the bizarre effects' and what he saw of his own reflection in the glass. 'So happily, indeed, did he succeed in the whole of

Self-portrait with a Friend by Raphael (1483–1520), c. 1519. The Italian, who was summoned to Rome by Pope Julius II, painted several likenesses of himself. (Musée du Louvre, Paris, France)

this work, that the reality was no less real than the painting', wrote Vasari in admiration; 'in it were seen the lustre of the glass, the reflection of every detail, and the lights and shadows, all so true and natural, that nothing more could have been hoped for from the human intellect'.

In Spain, El Greco projected himself into several religious paintings, most notably *The Burial of Count Orgaz* for the church of S. Tomé in Toledo. A fourteenth-century nobleman of extraordinary piety was at his death honoured by the descent from open heaven of Saints Stephen and Augustine, who lifted the body and placed it in the tomb. The painter portrayed himself among the distinguished company witnessing this miraculous scene.

Self-portrait by Sofonisba Anguissola (c. 1532–1625), late 1550s. Anguissola is one of the earliest women artists about whom anything is known. She has depicted herself as a painter, at work on a picture of the Virgin and Child. (Muzeum Zamek, Lancut, Poland)

The Artist at Work

It was with a new-found sense of their own status that painters began to portray themselves with the tools of their trade. One of the earliest self-portraits to show all the paraphernalia of painting — paintbrush, mahlstick and palette, and in this case a painting of the Virgin and Child to indicate the range of the artist's capabilities — was the work of a sixteenth-century woman painter, Sofonisba Anguissola. Her father, a nobleman of Cremona, had taken the unusual step of permitting her to be instructed in painting, at a time when training in any trade or profession was denied to women.

Describing her natural charms as well as her talent, both of which might be deduced from her self-portraits, Vasari wrote:

'Anguissola has shown greater application and better grace than any other woman of our age in her endeavours at drawing; she has

Self-portrait by Johannes Gumpp
(born 1626), 1646. The triple portrait
of the Austrian artist at his easel
shows him painting a portrait of himself from his reflection in a mirror.
(Galleria degli Uffizi, Florence, Italy)

thus succeeded not only in drawing, colouring and painting from
nature, and copying excellently from others, but by herself has created rare and very beautiful paintings'.

The image that Anguissola would have seen of herself in the glass was not
only converted into two dimensions but in reverse — as, today, the
number plate of a car travelling behind is seen in the driving-mirror.
Every right-handed painter, holding a paintbrush, book or any other
object and looking at his or her reflection, sees it held in the left hand.
Although all the facial features — including blemishes — appear to be on
the 'wrong' side, it is customary, in the case of an artist portraying himself
at work or with the attributes of painting, to correct only the position of
the hand, transferring the pencil or brush from one to the other. In some
instances, the hand is thought to have been based on that of a model
posing for the artist. In the process of engraving, the original image is
automatically reversed.

In the middle of the seventeenth century the Austrian artist Johannes
Gumpp produced a self-likeness, in a circular format, that illustrates in a
most inventive way how he painted his self-portrait. The device he used
was that of a triple image. He pictured himself from behind, looking at his
reflection in a mirror (which is visible by the viewer of the picture), and
making in paint a copy (which is also visible to the viewer) of his
reflection. The arrangement of the mirrors enabling him to see his own
back is not shown.

The two versions of his face are subtly different, a fact that is most
noticeable in the direction of the eyes, even though the head is positioned
at an identical angle. And the head on the canvas is slightly larger than the
one in the reflection, which would inevitably be slightly smaller than his

own head (the reflection always being smaller than the actual). In the foreground are a fiercely antagonistic dog and cat, perhaps indicating aspects of Gumpp's own character that he felt were at odds with each other.

A complex and much larger composition showing the artist at work is Velázquez's *Las Meniñas*. Painted in 1656, it depicts the infanta Margarita with, in the foreground, her *meniñas* (attendant noblewomen), her dog and her dwarfs. On the left the painter stands back from an enormous canvas, brush and palette in hand. On the back wall is an ebony-framed mirror, and in it the misty reflection of the Spanish king and queen. It is interesting that Jan van Eyck's wedding portrait of Giovanni Arnolfini and his wife, with the mirror a prominent feature, was in the Spanish royal collection when this was painted.

Las Meniñas may be understood in more than one way. Perhaps the princess and her entourage are in the room where Velázquez is working. As she rests from sitting for her portrait and is offered a little pot of chocolate by one of her maids of honour, her parents enter. The maid on the right prepares to curtsey, the painter and the gentleman in the doorway adopt attitudes of respect. All the principal figures are caught together at a single moment, responding to something that occurs outside the picture, approximately where the spectator would be.

Another interpretation is that the painting depicts the arrival on the scene of the infanta — perhaps unexpected — accounting for the frozen and attentive poses of the figures. The original title of the picture was *The Royal Family*, and this, clearly, is its subject. But what is the subject of the canvas on the easel? Philip IV and his queen or their daughter, who was at that time next in line to the throne?

In France, Poussin's self-portrait shows the artist not at work but in his studio, in front of three framed canvases and with one hand resting on his

Las Meniñas by Diego Rodriguez de Silva y Velázquez (1599–1660), c. 1657. The Spanish painter's picture of the royal family includes a portrait of himself behind a large-scale canvas, the subject of which is a mystery to the spectator. (Prado, Madrid, Spain)

portfolio. It was painted for his friend and patron, Paul Fréart de Chantelou, who was also the patron of Bernini. On the left is glimpsed the figure of a woman wearing a diadem, a detail from an allegorical painting. Much of his subject-matter in Rome, where he lived permanently after 1842, was based on classical themes.

Painter and Gentleman

The seventeenth century produced a number of portraits that show the artists as aristocrats or at least as fine gentleman, well dressed and secure in the position they enjoy in the social order. Three Flemish painters, in particular, show themselves in this light: Rubens, Jordaens and Van Dyck.

In about 1609 Rubens painted a picture celebrating his marriage to Isabella Brandt, the daughter of an influential and well-to-do Antwerp patrician. By then he had spent eight years in Italy, for most of that time in the service of Vincenzo Gonzaga, Duke of Mantua. His life at court had brought him affluence and taught him the manners of a nobleman. This is evident in his fashionable attire and in the confident bearing of the newly-wed couple under the honeysuckle. One hand rests on the hilt of a sword — a mark of his place in society — a finger pointing to the other hand, on which rests that of his bride.

Just over ten years later, Jordaens painted a portrait of himself with his family and this, too, pronounces the regard in which the artist is held. Lute in hand, one foot resting on the bar of a chair and balancing himself with a hand on its back, he represents an elegant figure. His nobility is emphasized by the low viewpoint: the spectator is put in the position of looking up to him.

Rubens and Isabella Brandt under the Honeysuckle by Peter Paul Rubens (1577–1640), c. 1609. The double portrait of the Flemish painter and his wife celebrates their marriage. (Alte Pinakothek, Munich, Germany)

Van Dyck, unlike Rubens and Jordaens, was primarily a portrait-painter. For a time he worked with Rubens in his studio, and he was undoubtedly influenced by the older master. The picture of himself at about the age of thirty has all the grace and style of his portraits of Italian and English patrons. He spent the last nine years of his life in England and was knighted by Charles I. He indicated rank through the pose of his sitters — the hand on the hip being a gesture of authority — the grandeur of the setting and costume details. Though renowned for flattering his sitters, he was at the same time sensitive to individual character and temperament, which he interpreted from the features and expression of the face.

Self-portrait by Anthony van Dyck (1599–1641), c. 1620. Van Dyck, who was born in Antwerp and worked in Italy and England, set standards in portrait-painting for the flattering likeness of the sitter. (Hermitage, St Petersburg, Russia)

Rembrandt by Rembrandt

Rembrandt, born in Leiden in Holland, painted at least forty self-portraits, and represented himself in some thirty etchings and a smaller number of drawings. He left an exceptional pictorial record of himself, from youth to old age and in different states of mind.

The earliest self-likenesses appear as heads in large-scale compositions, in the tradition that dates back to the Renaissance. He started the series of independent portraits as a young man in his early twenties, in around 1628, depicting himself close-up, in studies of facial expression, and in a variety of different costumes and roles. In the self-portrait wearing a plumed beret and mustard-coloured cloak the focus is on the jewel at the centre of his headdress and on the gold chain around his shoulders. In a full-length portrait of two years later he is in Oriental attire, wearing a turban and cloak, with a tasselled sash about the waist.

Self-portrait with Two Circles
by Rembrandt Harmensz. van Rijn
(1606–69), 1665–69. Rembrandt,
in his series of about forty painted
self-portraits, reveal not only the
changes in his appearance as he grew
older but also in the way he regarded
himself. (Kenwood House, London,
England)

Gradually, the principal interest would become his own face. He grew a moustache, and the thick tousle of hair turned grey. Lines appeared in his forehead, the features coarsened and his air of assurance was replaced by an anxious look. Simultaneously, his technique changed. The paint-surface became rougher with the use of impasto — dabs of thick paint — giving the paintings the appearance of being unfinished.

Rembrandt's wife Saskia, who appears in the picture of the tavern scene, died in 1642, and at about that time his popularity began to decline. By 1656 he was in financial difficulties and was forced to sell his art collection. With fewer commissions coming his way, he turned — now with greater depths of self-knowledge — to painting his own portrait.

The Collectors

Rembrandt lived at a time when art was regarded as a subject for serious study and discussion among groups of educated people, when artists were visited in their studios and works of art commissioned and bought by a growing number of people. Teniers the Younger's painting of the Archduke Leopold Wilhelm in his picture gallery (which includes a likeness of the artist) illustrates seventeenth-century aristocratic interest in collecting works of art. Charles I was another notable connoisseur and collector of the period.

Since the sixteenth century portraits of famous people — artists among them — had been greatly sought after. Rembrandt, who was internationally known and admired, may have produced as many self-portraits as he did partly to satisfy the demand from collectors. One of his pictures went to the collection of self-portraits belonging to Cardinal Leopoldo de' Medici.

Leopoldo's collection had begun with portraits of some of the great men of the Renaissance that had been brought together by Cosimo I de' Medici. Through purchases and gifts the collection grew, and from 1664 he commissioned artists such as Carlo Dolci to paint self-portraits. His interest lay not only in the likeness to the painters but in the fact that each one represented the style of that artist. In the Palazzo Pitti he had the pictures hung in chronological order, as a survey of the art of two centuries. Cosimo III, who became Grand Duke of Tuscany, doubled his uncle's collection of about eighty self-portraits and moved it to a special gallery in the Uffizi. Cosimo's children, in turn, made additions.

The Medici line in Florence died out in 1737, and during the rule of the dukes of Lorraine self-portraits by Jean-Etienne Liotard and Christian Seybold among others were sent to Florence by Francis, Duke of Lorraine (who in 1745 was elected Holy Roman Emperor) and his wife, Maria Teresa.

Later, foreign artists visiting Florence and copying works in the Galleria degli autoritratti were invited to donate works, and in this way self-portraits by Madame Vigée-Lebrun, Reynolds, Ingres, Leighton, Fantin-Latour and Sargent entered the collection. Many of the pictures reproduced in this book are in the Uffizi.

Autobiographical Art of the Eighteenth Century

The self-portraits in the collection founded by the cardinal do indeed illustrate the style of each artist, as he intended. And so, too, do the other paintings, drawings and prints illustrated here. From the eighteenth century are self-portraits by artists alaphabetically from William Aikman to Johann Zoffany and chronologically from Paolo Matteis's allegory of

Self-portrait by Christian Seybold (1690–1768), 1747. The close-up portrait of the German artist was one of the pictures sent to the Uffizi collection of self-portraits from Austria in the eighteenth century. (Galleria degli Uffizi, Florence, Italy)

painting of about 1710 to the portrait that was on Reynolds's easel when he died in 1792, by way of Hogarth, Gainsborough, Batoni, Chardin and other of the great names of the century.

During those years a number of pictures were produced that indicate some fact about the artist apart from his style of painting and what he looked like. Bernard Lens, in his miniature, showed himself as a miniaturist; Thomas Barker of Bath portrayed himself, with his patron, in the act of painting a landscape; Jacob More, similarly, depicted himself as a landscape painter; Antonio Ciocchi included his portrait in a still-life depicting objects he associated with himself; Liotard's costume exhibits his passion for the Near East, especially Turkey; Richard Cosway's drawing indicates his links with Freemasonry; George Morland painted himself as part of a rural scene, the subject of much of his work; Alexandre-François Desportes's self-portrait alludes to the chase, to the genre of painting in which he specialized; Rosalba Carriera, working at a portrait in pastel, reveals her favoured medium.

Women Artists by Themselves

Rosalba was one of several women artists to achieve a name for herself in the eighteenth century. Born in Venice, she had a great vogue among the English Grand Tourists. Unlike most of the others who are well known, she prospered without any particular connections at court.

In the sixteenth century, Anguissola's promotion of her artistic abilities through her self-portraits had taken her to the court of Philip II of Spain, where she was appointed a lady-in-waiting to teach painting to the young Elizabeth of Valois. Giovanna Fratellini, in the seventeenth century, was lady-in-waiting to the Grand Duchess of Tuscany. Anna Dorothea

Self-portrait by Jean-Etienne Liotard (1702–89). The Swiss artist illustrates his taste for all things Turkish in this pastel portrait of himself in Turkish dress. (Galleria degli Uffizi, Florence, Italy)

Lisiewska, in the eighteenth century, received many of her commissions from the Prussian court.

Marie-Louise-Elizabeth Vigée-Lebrun worked under the patronage of the French queen Marie-Antoinette and painted some thirty portraits of her. Because of her association with the Ancien Régime, Vigée-Lebrun found it expedient in 1789 to leave France with her child; together they are the subject of some of the most charming images of motherhood. Throughout her life her portraits commanded the highest prices, and her self-portrait in the Uffizi is one of the most frequently copied paintings in the collection. Angelica Kauffmann, who was some fourteen years Vigée-Lebrun's elder, and led a rather racier life, declined the position of court painter to King Ferdinand and Queen Caroline of Naples.

Learning to draw and paint formed part of the education of aristocratic and gentle ladies. The Archduchess Maria-Christina of the Austrian house of Habsburg is represented in this book by a portrait of herself at a spinning-wheel. She would have received lessons from a professional artist.

Paintings by nineteenth-century English amateurs include self-portraits by Mary Ellen Best and I. J. Willis, both of them seen at work in domestic interiors. Towards the end of the century women were accepted into art schools, and they were soon able to train, practise and exhibit as equals with men.

Self-portrait by Marie–Louise-Elizabeth Vigée-Lebrun (1755–1842), 1790. This is one of the pictures most frequently copied by the French artist herself and by visitors to the Uffizi. It was painted after she had fled from the Revolution in France. (Galleria degli Uffizi, Florence, Italy)

New Attitudes for the Nineteenth century

Jacques-Louis David held opposing political views to Madame Vigée-Lebrun and played an active part in the French Revolution of 1789. One of the self-portraits illustrated was painted while he was imprisoned following the fall of Robespierre, instigator of the Reign

Self-portrait by Caspar David
Friedrich (1774–1840), 1802.
Friedrich's work epitomizes the
Romantic Movement in Germany.
This drawing of himself is probably
from one of his sketchbooks.
(Kunsthalle, Hamburg, Germany)

of Terror. The expression on his face is tense, his sense of purpose
apparently undiminished, but at the same time there is an underlying
anxiety. This is the picture of a revolutionary, perplexed and no longer in
the prime of life.

Close in age to David was Francisco Goya. His portraits mock their
subjects and contain the sense of foreboding that is a characteristic of
Spanish painting. His figures are apt to express an air of pent-up unease.
In the portrait of himself wearing spectacles Goya seems almost to draw
back from his reflection in the mirror.

Samuel Palmer copied his mirror-image with appealing sincerity in the
close-up frontal drawing of himself as a young man of twenty-three. He
displays a similar hesitancy to Giovanni-Lorenzo Bernini in the
seventeenth-century Italian's drawing of himself. Palmer went on to create
an entirely personal vision of his native Kentish valley, the landscape
often in moonlight, in drawings, watercolours and prints that belong to
the English Romantic tradition. The landscapes by Caspar David
Friedrich that include the dark, cloaked figure of the artist, seen from
behind, are imbued with the mystery and sense of doom that typify
German Romantic art.

The painter regarded as the leader of nineteenth-century Romanticism
is Eugène Delacroix. He reacted against the style of Jean Auguste
Dominique Ingres, winner of the prestigious Prix de Rome and Professor
at the École des Beaux-Arts. While Ingres produced glossy, highly
finished works of great exactitude, Delacroix's technique was rougher
and more spontaneous. Individual brushstrokes were visible, shapes
were more important than outlines, and the effect was more expressive
of feeling.

Art and Photography

Courbet's dictum was, 'Painting is essentially a concrete art and can consist only of the representation of things both real and existing'. His painting of the studio was described by Delacroix in his journal as 'one of the most remarkable paintings of our times'. The huge canvas shows the painter working at his easel on a landscape, overlooked by a nude female model and surrounded by a large cast of characters, some of whom were his friends. A photograph of 1855, the date of the picture, proves that it is a lifelike portrait of the artist.

Both Delacroix and Courbet worked from photographs. Collections of photographic studies of the nude were produced at that time, and they encouraged artists to paint figures from real life instead of copying antique models. Degas and Manet belonged to the generation of artists who used photographs to help them in the composition of their pictures. The wet collodion process was invented in 1851, and, with the print on albumen-coated paper, portrait photography became available to all. Ingres, not surprisingly in view of the precision of his portrait style, condemned the elevation of photography to an art form, believing that it dealt a death blow to the painted portrait and art in general.

In fact, photography adjusted the nature and appeal of portrait-painting instead of destroying it. For some people the expectation was created of owning paintings of even greater photographic accuracy than before. But, because inexpensive photographic *cartes-de visite* were small, the figures posed and artificial-looking, and the image in black and white, portrait artists had leeway to introduce informality into their pictures, to use the bright colours made possible by the invention of aniline dyes and to create images that were summaries of the sitters' appearance and character

Self-portrait by Hilaire-Germain-Edgar Degas (1834–1917), 1855. Degas was of the generation of artists who were painting after the invention of photography. It taught him to compose pictures as 'snapshots' of a scene that would have extended beyond the edges of the canvas. (Musée d'Orsay, Paris, France)

rather than likenesses of a moment. Portraits on canvas were larger and more expensive than even the larger studio photographs, and they were therefore special. It was really the portrait miniature that had to compete with the photograph.

Impressionism and After

Monet, whose picture *Impression, Sunrise* gave its name to the movement, was concerned with the analysis of tone and colour, and the play of light and depths of shade on the landscape and buildings, with figures in the view playing a subsidiary role. Outline was more or less irrelevant, and accurate delineation unimportant. Particularly in his late work, shapes were suggested rather than stated. He painted his subjects in series at different times of day and in different lights.

Monet did paint a small number of self-likenesses, as did Pissarro. Renoir, who adopted Monet's light palette and free application of paint after they had worked together on the Seine, was more interested in figures than landscape, and in his early years made a living from portrait-painting. The self-portrait painted after the death of his favourite model is a touching image of a man growing old and sad.

Post-Impressionism and the Self-portrait

Cézanne adopted the Impressionists' technique and exhibited with them. His real interest, though, was in structure, and permanence rather than the fleeting effect. His approach was almost entirely objective, and in his self-portraits he treated his own face as a visual fact, no different from fruit arranged on a table or the mountainous bulk of Mont Saint-Victoire,

Self-portrait in a Casquette by Paul Cézanne (1839–1906), 1873 The free brushwork in this, one of a series of pictures for which the artist himself was the model, shows the influence of Impressionism. (Hermitage, St Petersburg, Russia)

which in his last years was so much before his eyes and in his mind. Conventional perspective was a hindrance rather than a help to him in conveying the feeling of solidity and depth.

In 1888, Van Gogh suggested to Gauguin that they exchanged pictures, as Japanese artists would often do, he said. The two masters of Post-Impressionism admired each other's work. Van Gogh was living at Arles in southern of France and Gauguin at Pont Aven in the north. The pictures they eventually swapped were self-portraits, likenesses of themselves and at the same time examples of their work, which it was hoped would increase understanding of each other. The paintings and the giving of them was an affirmation of friendship and of the artists' common interest in creating a 'poetic' mood through the use of colour.

Van Gogh's self-portraits are self-searching and self-critical. His life was made miserable by poverty, through the inability to sell his paintings. He was helped by his brother Theo, in whom he confided everything: his ideas, his intense sense of a mission that had to be accomplished, his struggles and triumphs and his loneliness. From Arles he wrote, 'the emotions are sometimes so strong that one works without being aware of working . . . the strokes come with a sequence and coherence like words in a speech or a letter'. His brushstrokes are to be read as the key to his emotions, and nowhere with a greater chance of understanding his tortured soul than in his self-portraits.

Gauguin felt that he would best be able to release and communicate his feelings if he were to learn about the ways of primitive peoples. In 1891, Gauguin left for the South Seas, returning to France only for a brief spell between 1893 and 1895. Though he reduced everything to simple forms and patterns, his painting was not naïve, but calculated to symbolize his ideas, to correspond to subjective states of mind.

Self-portrait by Vincent van Gogh (1853–90), 1889. The swirling paint of the background gives some idea of the painter's state of mind at the time. He had taken himself to an institution at Saint-Rémy. (Musée d'Orsay, Paris, France)

Self-portrait by Gino Severini
(1883–1966), 1913. The Italian used
his face and body as the basis for this
work, which is characteristic of the
Futurist style. (Private Collection)

Common Origins and Diversity in the Twentieth Century

By the end of the nineteenth century the scene was set for developments in
the twentieth century. Painters such as John Singer Sargent continued the
naturalistic tradition. He painted portraits of a similar technical virtuosity to Ingres', with the brushstroke concealed, and as elegant as paintings
by Thomas Lawrence. His talent was for portraying outward appearance.

The three principal Post-Impressionists released artists once and for all
from the obligation to copy nature, as taught in the academies and as in a
photograph. Cézanne's experiments with form led on to Cubism, to
Futurism as exemplified by Gino Severini's self-portrait and English
Vorticism as exemplified by Wyndham Lewis's. Van Gogh was the
forerunner of art that was concerned primarily with expressing emotion.
He paved the way for the self-disgust of Egon Schiele and sympathy-
seeking of Lovis Corinth. Chunky and flattened forms, and Primitivism in
various guises can be traced back to Gauguin. Max Beckmann's self-
portrait belongs in this category.

The self-likenesses by the Surrealists Salvador Dali and Paul Delvaux
reproduced here are details in and can be seen as 'signatures' — 'I was
there'. Lucian Freud's *Interior with Hand Mirror* is based on the ingenious
inclusion of the glass, and Mark Gertler's convex mirror-image has echoes
with the past. Picasso portrayed himself as an artist. Andy Warhol cultivated fame, as Rubens established for the viewer his position in society.

So, certain compositional devices recurred, and the artist still used his
portrait to explain himself and how he wished to be seen by others. But on
the whole it was his feelings and ideas that he wanted to explore. He found
that reproducing the features of his face that he saw in a mirror was not the
only way of describing his personality.

The Illustrations

The self-portraits illustrated on the following pages, which cover approximately five hundred years in the history of art in the West, are arranged in alphabetical order of artist. There are, therefore, some strange juxtapositions: Dufy next to Dürer, Picasso preceding Piero della Francesca. They answer the question, what did he or she look like? Or at the very least: how did they see themselves? In some cases they tell of the body and the soul.

Self-portrait by Pablo Picasso (1881–1973), 1906. While portraying himself as an artist, palette in hand in the conventional way, the Spaniard was beginning to develop a completely new style of painting that was to lead on to Cubism (Philadelphia Museum of Art, USA)

All works of art — and particularly portraits — contain an element of autobiography. They reveal something of their maker's personality and vision, their way of looking and thinking. Oscar Wilde, on the subject of the portrait in *The Picture of Dorian Gray*, wrote:

'every portrait that is painted with feeling is a portrait of the artist, not of the sitter. The sitter is merely the accident, the occasion. It is not he who is revealed by the painter, it is rather the painter who, on the coloured canvas, reveals himself'.

How much truer must this remark be when the painter and the sitter are one and the same?

JOHANN AACHEN (1552–1615), 1596
The German painter and draughtsman, one of the foremost artists at the court of the emperor Rudolf II in Prague,
portrays himself laughing and pointing a finger at his own reflection in the mirror. The woman with him is his wife,
whom he had married shortly before painting this double portrait. The deep shadows contrasting with areas
that are brightly lit are characteristic of Aachen's style.
(Kunsthistorisches Museum, Vienna, Austria)

WILLIAM AIKMAN (1682–1731), C. 1707
The self-likeness was the work of a young Scottish painter displaying his skills of control and close observation.
Aikman was later to develop a more decorative style, and he became a significant figure in the history of Scottish art.
(Scottish National Portrait Gallery, Edinburgh, Scotland)

ALESSANDRO ALLORI (1535–1621), c. 1555
The Florentine has depicted himself in the act of painting his self-portrait. His canvas is at right angles to the viewer,
who would be in the position of the mirror into which Allori is looking at his own reflection.
(Galleria degli Uffizi, Florence, Italy)

LAWRENCE ALMA-TADEMA (1836–1912), 1896
Born in Holland, Alma-Tadema settled in England in his mid-thirties. He became a Royal Academician in 1879 and was knighted in 1899. He chose to portray himself for the Uffizi collection of self-portraits as contemporary society viewed him: an affluent gentleman-painter in pince-nez, wearing a suit and jewelled tie-pin.
(Galleria degli Uffizi, Florence, Italy)

RUDOLPH VON ALT (1812–1905), 1890
Throughout his life, which spanned most of the nineteenth century, Alt recorded the architectural changes
to his native Vienna. He specialized in watercolours of landscapes, buildings and interiors, and was
so highly regarded that he was ennobled and made an honorary citizen of Vienna.
(Private Collection)

SOFONISBA ANGUISSOLA (c. 1532–1625), 1554
The daughter of an Italian nobleman, Anguissola is one of the first women painters about whom anything is known.
She painted a series of self-portraits, this one from her early years in Cremona.
Book in hand, she presents herself as a woman of learning.
(Kunsthistorisches Museum, Vienna, Austria)

SOFONISBA ANGUISSOLA (c. 1532–1625), late 1550s
The Italian artist here portrays herself as a still-demure but more confident character, at work on a painting of the
Virgin and Child. This is an early representation of the tools of a painter's trade, including a mahlstick,
a stick with a padded knob used to steady the hand when working on details.
(Muzeum Zamek, Lancut, Poland)

SOFONISBA ANGUISSOLA (c. 1532–1625), 1559
Anguissola is attired in this self-likeness in the dress she wore at the Spanish court, having been invited that year
to attend as a lady-in-waiting to Elizabeth of Valois, bride of Philip II. Vasari was fulsome in his praise
for the artist and her endeavours in 'drawing, colouring and painting'.
(Private Collection, Milan, Italy)

ANDREA APPIANI THE ELDER (1754–1817), c. 1794
In opposition to the formal constraints of his age, the Italian artist used his portraits to explore
the elimination of defined background detailing, concentrating instead on atmosphere
and the play of light and shadow, as shown in this portrayal of himself.
(Galleria degli Uffizi, Florence, Italy)

IL BACICCIO [GIOVANNI BATTISTA GAULLI] (1639–1709), 1667
The Italian artist, who has pictured himself in glamorous jacket and velvet cap, was the servant of the Catholic Church
in Rome. He executed spectacular religious frescoes, notably for the ceiling of the Gesù, the church of the Jesuits, and
practised as a portrait-painter, carrying out a series of portraits of cardinals and of seven successive popes.
(Galleria degli Uffizi, Florence, Italy)

LUDOLF BAKHUISEN (1630–1708), 1690s
Bakhuisen was a successful Dutch marine painter who was also a painter of portraits. This picture of himself combines these two types of subject; it expresses confidence in his position as an artist of national importance.
(Private Collection)

FRANCIS BACON (1909–92), 1970
The human figure was the principal subject for this individual and ultimately disturbing English artist, at a time
when Abstraction was the dominant style. Representations of people he knew well and self-likenesses
were reworked to create large-scale images of great intensity, without losing their original appearance.
(Private Collection © Estate of Francis Bacon/ARS, NY and DACS, London 1999)

BALTHUS [BALTHASAR KLOSSOWSKI DE ROLA] (1908–97), 1935
Balthus, a French painter of Polish extraction, gave this painting the ironic title *His Majesty the King of Cats*.
His best-known works have an erotic charge, and they created a scandal when they were first exhibited in Paris.
He may have intended the cat to represent his own sensuality. The cat in the picture used to visit him in his studio
in the rue Fürstenberg, coming in through the skylight.
(©ADAGP, Paris and DACS, London 1999)

THOMAS BARKER OF BATH (1767–1847), c. 1790
Self-portrait with his Preceptor Charles Spackman is the title of the picture.
Barker was sent by his patron Spackman to Rome for three years, afterwards returning to his native Bath.
He was celebrated as a painter of rustic scenes, some of which were copied on to Worcester china plates.
(Victoria Art Gallery, Bath and North East Somerset Council, England)

JAMES BARRY (1741–1806), C. 1800
The Irish artist was here working in bistre, a brown pigment prepared by boiling soot. Barry was a history painter
sympathetic to Reynolds's principles for history painting in the Grand Manner. He was appointed
Professor of Painting at the Royal Academy in 1783 but later expelled after internal quarrels.
(Ashmolean Museum, Oxford, England)

POMPEO BATONI (1708–87), 1773–74
As the most celebrated and notoriously proud Italian painter of his day, Batoni is remembered for his many portraits of compelling likeness of visitors on the Grand Tour. This self-portrait was unfinished at his death, when it was sold by his widow to the Uffizi, for which it was originally intended.
(Galleria degli Uffizi, Florence, Italy)

FRÉDÉRIC BAZILLE (1841–1870), 1867
Family Reunion, as the painting is called, shows the painter and his family on the terrace of the Bazille house, which was near Montpellier in France. The figures appear frozen at a single moment in time, having no communication with each other. It is as if they had been caught with all but the painter's father looking directly at a camera. Bazille, with his long, thin face and dark hair, is at the extreme left of the family group, with his cousin Monsieur des Hours standing beside him. (Musée du Louvre, Paris, France)

MARY BEALE (1632–99), c. 1664–68
In the self-portrait of the English artist as a shepherdess, with her son Charles in attendance, there is nothing
to indicate her profession. This is one of several likenesses of herself that she painted
as practice for allegorical and mythological subjects.
(Private Collection)

AUBREY BEARDSLEY (1872–98), c. 1892
Beardsley's pen-and-ink drawing of himself shows a cadaverous young man with lank hair, large ears
and dark shadows under the eyes. The effects of tuberculosis were already evident in the face of the young
artist and illustrator, who in his short life became a leading figure of the English *fin de siècle*.
(British Museum, London, England)

AUBREY BEARDSLEY (1872–98), 1896
In the engraving Beardsley stands with his pen under his arm, tethered by the ankles to a herm
of the god Pan, illustrating his allegiance to pagan rather than Christian values.
An expurgated version appeared in *The Savoy* magazine.
(Private Collection)

MAX BECKMANN (1884–1950), 1925
Usually presenting himself as an urbane city-dweller, this important German painter's
large and ambitious figure paintings depict modern life as theatre or cabaret,
with ambiguous and disturbing imagery. He sought to express emotional states in his
traditional compositions and formats of portraiture, religious works and landscapes.
(Christie's Images, London, England/© DACS 1999)

SIMON BENING (c. 1483–1561), c. 1540
The Benings were a fourteenth- and fifteenth-century family of illustrators.
The self-portrait is from a Book of Hours, used by lay people for private devotion;
it alludes to the artist's work and to his personal devoutness.
(Victoria & Albert Museum, London, England)

GIOVANNI-LORENZO BERNINI (1598–1680), c. 1615–19
The Italian artist painted himself here as a young man. The detail is concentrated in the face, his lace collar and his
hand being more loosely rendered. The creator and principal exponent of the Baroque style, his reputation was based on
his work as a sculptor and architect; he painted more than 150 pictures 'for his pleasure and as a pastime'.
(National Gallery of Victoria, Melbourne, Australia, Everard Studley Miller Bequest)

GIOVANNI-LORENZO BERNINI (1598–1680), c. 1630
The drawing is in black and red chalk with traces of white on paper. The Italian artist probably did this drawing as a
preparatory study, and in style it is closely related to his painted portraits. Bernini saw portraiture as an opportunity to
portray the psychological presence of the sitter, and this drawing of himself is an exercise in that approach.
(Ashmolean Museum, Oxford, England)

GIOVANNI-LORENZO BERNINI (1598–1680), c. 1641
The thinning hair and loosening skin are among the unmistakable signs of aging in this self-portrait of the great master
of the Baroque, executed in red and black chalk on paper. A man of deep religious conviction and piety,
he is said to have had a difficult and stormy temperament.
(Ashmolean Museum, Oxford, England)

Mary Ellen Best (1809–91), 1837–9
The watercolour is of the English provincial artist in her
painting-room in York. She was an amateur painter who
also worked to commission, specializing in portraits and
gentle domestic scenes.
(York City Art Gallery, England)

FERDINANDO GALLI BIBIENA (1647–1743), c. 1680
This is the self-likeness of an Italian painter best known for his designs for architecture and the theatre;
it was his talent in these areas that won him favour with the Duke of Parma and Piacenza.
He displays his status at court by focusing attention on his wig and sumptuous apparel.
(Galleria degli Uffizi, Florence, Italy)

ANNA BILINSKA (1857/58–93), 1887
The Polish artist portrays herself as the painter, with a handful of paintbrushes, and as the model,
posing against the neutral-coloured backcloth often to be found in artists' studios.
The embroidery of her apron is carefully picked out.
(National Museum, Cracow, Poland)

UMBERTO BOCCIONI (1882–1916), 1908
The Italian artist moved from Rome to Milan in 1907
and here depicts himself in an urban scene, probably a
housing estate on the edge of the city. Traditional
images of nature are replaced with buildings, one still
partly scaffolded, giving a sense of newness and
modernity typical of Futurist works.
(Pinacoteca di Brera, Milan, Italy).

UMBERTO BOCCIONI (1882–1916), 1909
This self-portrait by the Italian painter and sculptor shows the energy and dynamism
that characterize his work as a leading figure of Futurism. Lines are strongly and quickly drawn in ink
over a background of deeply coloured watercolour.
(Private Collection)

Pierre Bonnard (1867–1947), 1929
In 1929 Bonnard went to an exhibition of Chardin's work in Paris; the Frenchman's self-portrait
done in that year may represent his reflections on the earlier artist's portrait of himself
wearing round pince-nez. The drawing is coloured in watercolour and gouache.
(Private Collection/© ADAGP, Paris and DACS, London 1999)

LÉON-JOSEPH-FLORENTIN BONNAT (1833–1922), 1890s
Portraits by Bonnat typically show the influence of Van Dyck and Velázquez, whose work he saw in the Prado
when, as a young man, he was studying in Madrid. Here the French painter was more interested in portraying himself
as a fashionable and successful artist than in indicating much about his character.
(Musée Bonnat, Bayonne, France)

VIKTOR BORISOV-MUSATOV (1870–1905), 1898
After his four years in Paris the Russian artist used rich, bright colour but infused the high summer landscape
with a mood of romantic nostalgia. He is a shadowy presence, in his working smock,
his sister Elena pictured in the costume of an earlier, more innocent time.
(State Russian Museum, St Petersburg, Russia)

HIERONYMUS BOSCH (c. 1450–1516), c. 1504
This is a detail from the right wing of Bosch's triptych with *The Garden of Earthly Delights* as the centre panel.
Bosch, born in northern Brabant, was here at his most frenetic, dealing with a favourite subject:
the folly of mankind and the consequences of sin.
(Prado, Madrid, Spain)

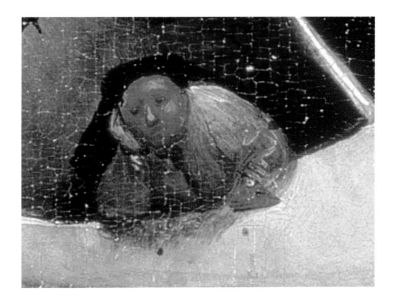

DETAIL:
The figure leaning on his elbow, at the edge of the broken shell inside the body of the monster, is
the artist himself contemplating, with eyes closed, his own hell.

SANDRO BOTTICELLI (1444/45–1510), early 1470s
The Italian Renaissance painting of *The Adoration of the Magi* includes a portrait of the artist himself
and the supposed portraits in profile of two members of the all-powerful Medici family:
Lorenzo, the figure in the foreground on the left, and his brother Giuliano,
the dark-haired figure with his head bowed in the middle ground on the right.
(Galleria degli Uffizi, Florence, Italy)

DETAIL
Botticelli's self-portrait is from the extreme right-hand side of the panel painting.
The full-length figure is the most prominent among those who face away
from the Madonna and Child and look out of the picture towards the viewer.

MARC THÉODORE BOURRIT (1735–1815), c. 1770
The Swiss artist looks up from reading his book and addresses the viewer's gaze
in an unnerving and watchful manner. The skilful use of watercolour heightened with white
enhances the impression of crumpled clothing.
(Private Collection)

THOMAS SHOTTER BOYS (1803–74), 1842
Born in London, the painter and printmaker belonged to the Anglo-French picturesque movement: he specialized in
watercolour townscapes of Paris and London. In *The Tower of London and Mint from Tower Hill* Boys portrays himself
as a rather portly figure sketching in the midst of the hustle and bustle of London street life.
(Guildhall Library, Corporation of London, England)

WILLEM VAN DEN BROECK (1520–79), 1564
Jan van den Broeck was a Flemish painter who had three sons: two were painters and Willem was a sculptor,
his work including still-extant statues for Antwerp Cathedral. He has pictured himself here
working on a wax portrait medallion.
(Kunsthistorisches Museum, Vienna, Austria)

Ford Madox Brown (1821–93), 1855
The Last of England was the most famous of all emigration pictures — a burning issue in Victorian times.
Inspired by the departure of the sculptor Thomas Woolner for Australia, Brown considered emigrating himself.
The models for the picture were the artist and his wife Emma, who sat outside in all weathers
so Brown could capture the colour of cold skin.
(Birmingham Museums and Art Gallery, England)

FORD MADOX BROWN (1821–93), 1877
William Michael Rossetti, Dante Gabriel's brother, described his first meeting with Brown: 'He was a vigorous-looking
man, with a face full of insight and purpose; thick straight brown hair, fair skin, well-coloured visage, bluish eyes,
broad brow, square and rather high shoulders, slow and distinct articulation. His face was good-looking
as well as fine; but less decidedly handsome, I think, than it became towards the age of forty.'
(Fogg Art Museum, Harvard University, Cambridge, USA, Bequest of Grenville L. Winthrop)

KARL PAVLOVICH BRYULLOV (1799–1852), 1848
A young prodigy from St Petersburg, the Russian artist settled in Rome, where he became an outstanding
portrait-painter of visiting Russian aristocrats. He presented his one large-scale history painting,
The Last Day of Pompeii, to the Emperor Nicholas I, and this briefly made him famous throughout Europe.
(State Russian Museum, St Petersburg, Russia)

Francesco Cairo (1607–65), c. 1632
Cairo, court painter at Turin and master of the dramatic devotional painting, made this self-portrait at about the age
of twenty-five. A simple head and shoulders composition, it is a highly atmospheric work. Cairo's typically muted
and subtle palette emphasizes the look of intense concentration on his face.
(Galleria degli Uffizi, Florence, Italy)

MICHELANGELO MERISI DA CARAVAGGIO (1571–1610), c. 1593
The Italian painter's self-likeness as a 'Sick Bacchus' aptly describes the volatile and revolutionary character who
rejected the European tradition of idealization of the human form in favour of frank realism. His use of models from
the Roman streets for sacred characters in religious paintings both scandalized and excited patrons.
(Galleria Borghese, Rome, Italy)

MICHELANGELO MERISI DA CARAVAGGIO (1571–1610), c. 1597–98
Thought to be a self-portrait of the Italian artist as Bacchus, this picture was only rediscovered
in the basement of the Uffizi in 1916. It shows off Caravaggio's skill as a portrait-painter and painter of still-life.
His bold, naturalistic style was enormously influential throughout Europe.
(Galleria degli Uffizi, Florence, Italy)

FELICE CARENA (1879–1966), 1930
Painted comparatively late in the Italian artist's career, the Symbolist manner of his early years had taken on an
edge of realism. He here contrasts the reticence of his own advancing age with the confidence of youth.
(Museo Civico Rivoltello, Trieste, Italy)

Rosalba Carriera (1675–1757), 1709
The Venetian artist depicts herself working on a portrait of her sister, and assistant, Giovanna.
She is working in pastels, sticks of compressed chalk, which was her favourite medium
and the one used for the self-portrait.
(Galleria degli Uffizi, Florence)

RAMON CASAS (1866–1932), 1897
The Catalan painter, the taller figure on the right, portrays himself here on a tandem with Pere Romeu.
The picture was painted while Casas was living in Paris and concentrating in his painting
on expressing the poetry and energy in everyday scenes. Casas produced commercial posters,
and the immediate impact that was required in that art form is evident in this work.
(Museo d'Art Modern, Barcelona, Spain)

NICCOLÒ CASSANA (1659–1713), c. 1683
Probably painted at the time he enrolled in the guild of Venetian painters, this self-image was sent by the young
Italian portrait-painter, seeking a court position in Florence, to Grand Prince Ferdinand de' Medici.
Cassana did indeed receive his patronage after they met, and they became friends five years later.
(Galleria degli Uffizi, Florence, Italy)

GIACOMO CERUTI (1698–1767) c. 1740
The Italian was known as '*Il Pitocchetto*' because he painted a number of pictures of vagrants
and the poor (*pitocchi* means 'vagabond'). In these, as in this portrait in which he carefully
recorded his own features, he worked in dark tones.
(Pinacoteca di Brera, Milan, Italy)

PAUL CÉZANNE (1839–1906), 1872–73
In *Pastoral*, a modernized homage to the Old Masters and to Manet, the French artist has placed himself, reclining, at the centre of a classical pastoral idyll and gazing at the naked female figures. He considered the study of nature, in a structural and enduringly solid manner, essential to art.
(Musée d'Orsay, Paris, France)

PAUL CÉZANNE (1839–1906), 1873
Executed in a sombre, traditional palette, this self-likeness of the French artist, his face dramatically lit, is executed in
the characteristic thick, impasto paint that he used to build form. The picture was done in the Paris studio of his artist
friend Armand Guillaumin, and a view of the Seine by Guillaumin is depicted in the background.
(Musée d'Orsay, Paris, France)

PAUL CÉZANNE (1839–1906), 1873
In a working man's *casquette*, with long hair and beard, this self-likeness of the French artist displays new Impressionist influences in its use of looser, more fluid brushstrokes and a brighter palette. It continues his exploration and belief in the inalienable relationship of colour and form.
(Hermitage, St Petersburg, Russia)

PAUL CÉZANNE (1839–1906), 1881–82
This is a more self-assured and artistically confident self-image in which the French artist does not portray
the uncouthness he knew he displayed when compared with his more elegant fellow artists.
He is dressed in a bourgeois suit, juxtaposed with the traditional artisan's cap,
the picture invoking comparison with self-portraits by Rembrandt.
(Neue Pinakothek, Munich, Germany)

PAUL CÉZANNE (1839–1906), 1885–87
The French painter has declared his identity as an artist with confidence in this self-image. Bare-headed and with an open shirt, his attention is turned to his work on the easel; in his hand he holds his palette and brushes.
(Bührle Collection, Zurich, Switzerland)

PAUL CÉZANNE (1839–1906), 1890–94
In a conventional pose for self-portraits, and one used often by the French artist, he displays the sharp outlining of forms that merge in colour, a style he developed working in the bright light of Provence. Having by this time received a large inheritance, Cézanne is the image of the bourgeois, and on the brink of artistic success.
(Bridgestone Museum of Art, Tokyo, Japan)

JEAN-BAPTISTE-SIMÉON CHARDIN (1699–1779), 1771
Chardin is regarded as the greatest French painter of still-life before Cézanne. At the end of his life
he turned to pastel portraits, of which this is one. It was exhibited at the 1775 Salon
alongside another self-portrait and a portrait of his wife.
(Musée du Louvre, Paris, France)

MILLY CHILDERS (active 1888–1920), 1889
Holding her head on one side, the English artist stops work and holds her brush and palette in the same hand to
appraise the portrait of herself. This represents precisely her serious attitude towards painting.
(City Art Gallery, Leeds Museums and Galleries, England)

LUDOVICO CARDI CIGOLI (1559–1613), c. 1607
The Italian Cigoli was famous in his native Florence and in Rome for his painting and architecture;
also as a poet, orator and musician. His fragile health and melancholy temperament are conveyed
in this self-portrait, with its soft use of warm colour to depict the fur cap and lace collar.
(Galleria degli Uffizi, Florence, Italy)

ANTONIO CIOCCHI (1732–92), c. 1789
The Italian was a master of the genre of *trompe l'oeil*, which tricks the eye into believing in the reality
of the objects depicted. He has painted a corner of his studio with items of significance to him.
The compasses may be a Masonic reference.
(Galleria degli Uffizi, Florence, Italy)

DETAIL
Among the still-life details in the painting is a self-portrait. A mysteriously pointing finger
breaks out of its own dimension and into the space of the room, confusing the illusion.

LOVIS CORINTH (1858–1925), 1920
After the German artist suffered a stroke in 1911, causing partial paralysis on one side of his body and some
distortion of his facial features, he became increasingly introverted. This lithograph is one of many
examinations of his own face that are revealing of his anxious personality.
(Wolseley Fine Arts, London, England)

Lovis Corinth (1858–1925), c. 1920–21
Corinth began to make prints in the 1920s, this one a drypoint done in the latter part of his life. He held a patriotic
belief that the First World War would bring about the rebirth of German art and afterwards argued vehemently
against the art of the international avant-garde and its influence in his own country.
(Wolseley Fine Arts, London, England)

LOVIS CORINTH (1858–1925), 1924
The German artist customarily painted a portrait of himself on his birthday, 21st July.
This rugged self-image was done at his house on the Walchensee on his sixty-sixth birthday.
(Bayerische Staatsgemäldesammlungen, Munich, Germany)

JEAN-BAPTISTE-CAMILLE COROT (1796–1875), 1834
Portraying himself here with brush and palette, the French painter's commitment to his career as an artist is clear.
Corot was asked to contribute a portrait of himself to the Uffizi's self-portrait collection,
and the picture was donated by his family after his death.
(Galleria degli Uffizi, Florence, Italy)

ANTONIO ALLEGRI CORREGGIO (c. 1489/94–1534), c. 1525–30
Little known in his own lifetime, the Italian painter, of whom this may be a self-portrait, was revered by subsequent
generations of artists. His influence centred on his soft use of colour and paint, the dramatic excitement
of his religious works and the sensuality of his mythological and allegorical paintings.
(Courtauld Gallery, London, England)

JAN COSSIERS (1600–71), c. 1660
The early work of this Flemish painter and draughtsman consisted of genre scenes, especially with fortune-tellers and gypsies. In his later career Cossiers concentrated on historical pictures with religious themes. The self-portrait is in chalk and black ink on paper. He became one of Antwerp's most prominent artists in the second half of the seventeenth century.
(Ashmolean Museum, Oxford, England)

RICHARD COSWAY (1742–1821), c. 1800
The English artist Cosway supplemented his income by dealing and was himself a connoisseur,
building up a fine collection of works of art and curiosities, and an extensive library.
This drawing, in charcoal and watercolour on paper, depicts Cosway in a manner
suggesting links with the arcane learning of the Masons.
(Galleria degli Uffizi, Florence, Italy)

RICHARD COSWAY (1742–1821), 1805–10
This work in watercolour on ivory, with its limited range of colours, is typical of this English artist.
He was the most famous miniature painter of his day, portraying the beautiful and the fashionable,
and he became Principal Painter to the Prince Regent.
(Fitzwilliam Museum, University of Cambridge, England)

GUSTAVE COURBET (1819–77), c. 1846
This self-portrait of the young French painter with 'dangerously' socialist ideas was later described as
'the portrait of a man filled with ideals'. Both the pose and the manner in which the picture is painted
demonstrate Courbet's early debt to Venetian painting.
(Musée d'Orsay, Paris, France)

GUSTAVE COURBET (1819–77), 1854
Known as *Bonjour Monsieur Courbet*, the painting shows the artist's arrival in Montpellier, staff in hand and
with a box of painting materials wrapped in a coat on his back. He is greeted by his friend Alfred Bruyas,
who has doffed his hat in welcome. Behind stands Bruyas's servant Calas, in an attitude of respect.
(Musée Fabre, Montpellier, France)

GUSTAVE COURBET (1819–77), 1855
The full title of Courbet's imposing picture is
*The Interior of my Studio, a Real Allegory Determining
a Phase of Seven Years in my Artistic Life*; it measures
141 x 235 inches (359 x 598 cm). 'In it,' he wrote,'are the
people who thrive on life and those who thrive on death;
it is society at its best, its worst, and its average.' At the
centre of the canvas is the artist, 'showing the Assyrian
profile of my head'. The painting on the easel is a
landscape of the valley of the Loue; leaning on the back
of his chair is a nude model and two to the right of her
is a portrait in profile of Alfred Bruyas. There are
thirty figures in all, including other of his friends as
well as characters he had come across and painted from
memory, such as the Jew on the extreme left.
(Musée d'Orsay, Paris, France)

AELBERT CUYP (1620–91), c. 1640
The title of the painting is *A Wooded Landscape with the Artist Sketching*. Cuyp was considered one of the most important seventeenth-century Dutch landscape artists, many of whose paintings include figures and horses. He had many followers, and his pictures were much sought after by collectors.
(Private Collection)

SALVADOR DALI (1904–89), 1962
The talented, prolific and flamboyantly eccentric Spanish Catalan painter has included in *The Ecumenical Council*
his usual model, his wife Gala; also, outside the vortex of this hallucinatory religious work, his own self-likeness. This
traditional image of the artist at his easel reflects Dali's concern with the established practice and skills of the artist.
(Salvador Dali Museum, St Petersburg, Florida, USA

JACQUES LOUIS DAVID (1748–1825), 1790–91
David was the most prominent painter of the Neoclassical movement in France. All self-portraits by David are
different from portraits of him by other artists because of one distinctive feature. He had a tumour on his left cheek
at the corner of his mouth, which grew larger with age and finally caused that side of his face to be deformed.
Using a mirror to paint himself, the deformity always appears in reverse, on his right cheek.
(Musée du Louvre, Paris, France)

JACQUES LOUIS DAVID (1748–1825), 1794–5

This picture is undated but, according to the artist's grandson, it was painted when David was imprisoned in the hôtel des Fermes. His fortunes had fallen with Robespierre in the debacle of the ninth Thermidor and he was incarcerated in the autumn of 1794 until the following year, when the Directory released him. David was a great, if somewhat immodest, teacher: 'I founded a brilliant school, I painted pictures that the whole of Europe came to study.'

(Galleria degli Uffizi, Florence, Italy)

HILAIRE-GERMAIN-EDGAR DEGAS (1834–1917), 1855
Degas was the son of an Italian-French father and a French Creole mother, which would explain some features
of his appearance. He studied at the Ecole des Beaux-Arts in Paris, where he was a pupil of Ingres.
Early portraits such as this suggest that he would follow in the academic tradition of his master.
(Musée d'Orsay, Paris, France)

HILAIRE-GERMAIN-EDGAR DEGAS (1834–1917), C. 1863
The manner in which Degas has cropped his hat at the side of the canvas is characteristic of the French artist's work,
reflecting his interest in photography. It illustrates the idea of an artwork capturing a segment of reality rather than
being of a subject chosen and confined within a frame. The 'real' is shown to extend beyond the edge of the picture.
(Museu Calouste Gulbenkian, Lisbon, Portugal)

HILAIRE-GERMAIN-EDGAR DEGAS (1834–1917), c. 1865
In this unfinished painting Degas portrays himself with the painter Evariste de Valernes. Indicating their shared
affection for Rome, the French artist has made it seem as if they are on a balcony overlooking the Forum.
The contrast in their poses, each man sunk in reflection, casts a strange inference on the nature of their friendship.
(Musée d'Orsay, Paris, France)

FERDINAND-EUGÈNE-VICTOR DELACROIX (1798–1863), c. 1839
This many-talented Frenchman was a painter, draughtsman, lithographer, writer and art critic, the embodiment of
Romanticism in the visual arts. He was inspired by Constable, Géricault, Michelangelo, Poussin and Rubens. Such
was his success that at one time he employed up to thirty assistants. Delacroix's approach to painting called on
literature for his subject-matter, science for his study of colour relationships, photography to study form.
(Musée du Louvre, Paris, France)

PAUL DELVAUX (1897–1994), 1938
The painting by the Belgian artist, called *The Sleeping Town*, has the hallucinatory quality that is characteristic of his
work. The painter appears on the left of the picture, observing the moonlit scene. Together with Magritte,
Delvaux was a major exponent of Surrealism in Belgium, and this picture was painted
in the year he took part in the International Surrealist Exhibition in Paris.
(Private Collection/© Foundation P Delvaux – St Idesbald, Belgium/DACS, London 1999)

MAURICE DENIS (1870–1943), 1916
The French painter depicted himself in this painting in front of the Prieuré. It dates from the later part
of his career when he had become committed to the revival of religious art.
It illustrates his interest in flat form and non-naturalistic colour.
(Galleria degli Uffizi, Florence, Italy/©ADAGP, Paris and DACS, London 1999)

ALEXANDRE-FRANÇOIS DESPORTES (1661—1743), 1699
The title of the picture is *Self-portrait of a Hunter*. Desportes was French artist celebrated for his pictures of dogs
and game in the Flemish tradition. He was court painter to Jan Sobieski in Poland until the king's death
and was later appointed by Louis XV of France painter of the royal hunt and kennels.
Desportes was considered eccentric as he chose to paint *en plein-air*.
(Musée du Louvre, Paris, France)

ARTHUR DEVIS (c. 1711–87), c. 1737
Devis was the English master of small conversation pieces depicting the middle class, his genteel style appealing to
eighteenth-century collectors with newly acquired wealth. He is known to have painted four self-portraits,
of which this is the earliest. He is shown here at the beginning of his career as a portrait-painter,
following the disbanding of the studio of his teacher Peter Tillemans in 1733.
(Harris Museum and Art Gallery, Preston, England)

ARTHUR DEVIS (c. 1711–87), 1742
When this portrait was relined in 1936 a small piece of card was found between the canvas and the stretcher,
inscribed 'I Give this Picture to my Grandson Thomas Devis'. Obviously inspired by his grandfather,
Thomas went on to become a painter of portraits and fancy pictures.
(Harris Museum and Art Gallery, Preston, England)

ARTHUR DEVIS (c. 1711–87), c. 1754
Devis exhibited at the Free Society of Artists between 1761 and 1780, and later became the President.
A new direction in Devis's painting is evident here, as he began to use strong *chiaroscuro* (light and shade)
in the lighting of his figures, a technique later adopted by Joseph Wright of Derby.
(Harris Museum and Art Gallery, Preston, England)

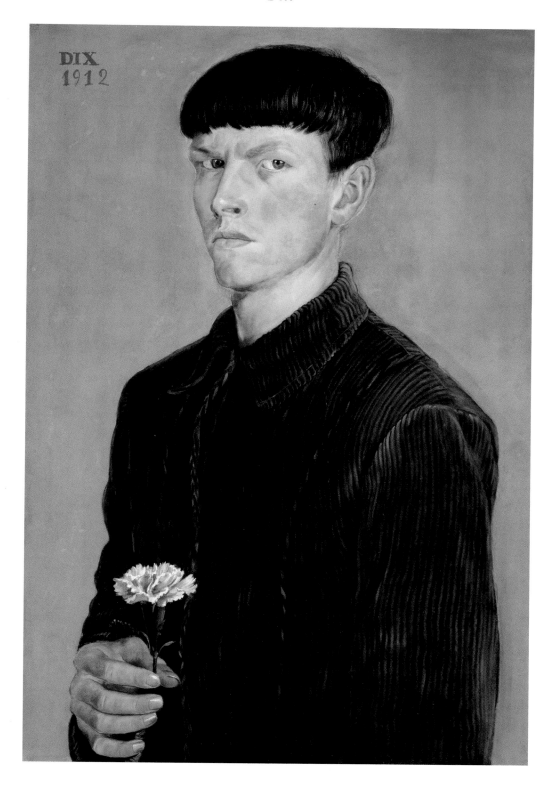

OTTO DIX (1891–1969), 1912
At this early stage in his career Dix was employed as a mural painter. The German taught himself to paint in tempera
and oils in the manner of Dürer and the artists of the northern European Renaissance.
(The Detroit Institute of Arts, USA, Gift of Robert H. Tannahill/©DACS 1999)

CARLO DOLCI (1616–87), 1674
The Florentine painter here depicted himself from the side and from the front, in town and country dress,
and both with and without spectacles, using the device of a work of art within a work of art.
(Galleria degli Uffizi, Florence, Italy)

GERARD [GERRIT] DOU (1613–75), 1650
The Dutchman was a pupil and companion of Rembrandt, who obviously influenced Dou's
experiments with *chiaroscuro* (light and shade). Dou was the founder of the Leiden *fijnschilders*
(fine painters), who specialized in small, highly detailed pictures.
(Cheltenham Art Gallery & Museum, England)

CHARLES ALTAMONT DOYLE (1832–93), C. 1885–93
The British artist produced the sinister *Self-portrait: A Meditation* when he was confined to the Montrose Royal
Lunatic Asylum suffering from epilepsy and alcoholism. John Doyle, the political cartoonist, was his father; Richard
Doyle, also a fairy painter, was his brother; Sir Arthur Conan Doyle, the creator of Sherlock Holmes, was his son.
(Victoria & Albert Museum, London, England)

RAOUL DUFY (1877–1953), c. 1945
Influenced by Impressionism and the Fauves, Dufy developed a highly distinctive and original use of line and colour,
as shown in this late self-portrait. The French painter and printmaker characteristically used
lively, fluid marks of the brush and vivid colours.
(Musée des Beaux-Arts, Le Havre, France/©ADAGP, Paris and DACS, London 1999)

KAREL DUJARDIN (1626–78), 1662
The Dutch painter was best known for his Italianate landscapes of cattle in a meadow, and herdsmen and
travellers outside a rural inn. As the *Self-portrait Holding a Roemer* shows, he was also
a fine portrait-painter, with a highly sensitive interpretation of light and shade.
(Johnny van Haeften Gallery, London, England)

ALBRECHT DÜRER (1471-1528), 1484
The drawing, in silverpoint on paper, was executed when the German artist was helping in his father's
goldsmith's shop in Nuremberg. The inscription reads, 'This I drew, using a mirror;
it is my own likeness in the year 1484, when I was still a child.'
(Graphische Sammlung Albertina, Vienna, Austria)

ALBRECHT DÜRER (1471–1528), 1493
The picture of the artist holding a thistle is believed to be one of the earliest independent painted self-portrait
in northern European art. The inscription reads, 'Things with me fare as ordained from above',
indicating Dürer's submission to the will of God.
(Musée du Louvre, Paris, France)

ALBRECHT DÜRER (1471–1528), 1498
Now five years older than in the previous picture, Dürer portrays himself dressed in the height of fashion,
with a moustache and beard, and his hair curled and falling to the shoulders.
The artist doubtless took pride in his own appearance.
(Prado, Madrid, Spain)

ALBRECHT DÜRER (1471–1528), 1511
The great altarpiece of *The Adoration of the Holy Trinity* was commissioned by Matthäus Landauer for the chapel
of a home for old and indigent men. The elderly donor appears as the figure on the left being encouraged by
a red-robed cardinal to participate in the event.
(Kunsthistorisches Museum, Vienna, Austria)

DETAIL
Dürer's self-portrait is in the foreground of the landscape at the bottom right-hand corner of the altarpiece.
He stands alone, next to a memorial tablet bearing his monogram and the date.

ANTHONY VAN DYCK (1599–1641), c. 1620
The Flemish artist is famous for his portraits of the English aristocracy and his role as a court painter.
Van Dyck's father died in 1622, leaving his eldest son to care for his siblings.
The grief and despair the artist felt is symbolized by the broken column behind him.
(Hermitage, St Petersburg, Russia)

ANTHONY VAN DYCK (1599–1641), c. 1635
Van Dyck did a series of double portraits, which show a debt to Raphael whom he greatly admired; he has here
adopted for himself the pose of Raphael's friend. The other sitter in Van Dyck's picture is Sir Endymion Porter.
Van Dyck's portraits were intended to flatter the subjects, making them look both distinguished and intelligent.
(Prado, Madrid, Spain)

THOMAS COWPERTHWAIT EAKINS (1844–1916), 1902
Now regarded as one of the greatest American painters of his period, Eakins's contemporary reputation was affected by
his controversial teaching of anatomy to women students and the non-aristocratic subjects of his portraits. The direct
and powerful gaze of his self-image is coupled with his skilful but conservative style.
(National Academy of Design, New York, USA)

RICHARD EURICH (1903–92), 1938
First struck by the awesome beauty of the sea at the age of fifteen, this Yorkshire-born English artist gained public
recognition for his dramatic depictions of sea battles of the Second World War. As with this self-portrait,
his atmospheric landscapes and seascapes, were constructed with serious, strong modelling of paint.
(Bradford Art Galleries and Museums, England/© Courtesy of the Eurich Estate/Bridgemn Art Library, London)

JAN VAN EYCK (c. 1390–1441), 1434
It is believed that the male figure represents Giovanni Arnolfini, one of the many Italians resident in Bruges,
the European centre of banking in the fifteenth century, and that the female figure is his wife,
from another Italian family of traders and financiers who had been long settled in the North.
Van Eyck may have been commissioned to paint the picture to celebrate their marriage.
(National Gallery, London, England)

DETAIL

On the back wall, in the picture, is a convex mirror, unusually large and elaborate for the time with the ten roundels
minutely depicting scenes of the Passion. In the mirror are reflected the back view of the couple and two men entering
the room. The man in blue raises his left arm, exchanging a greeting with Giovanni Arnolfini.
Above is the inscription '*Johannes de eyck fuit hic*' (Jan van Eyck was present),
and it is therefore supposed that the man in the reflection is Van Eyck himself.

IGNACE HENRI JEAN FANTIN-LATOUR (1836–1904), 1859
A series of youthful self-portraits mark the beginning of this French artist's painting from life; his apprenticeship
had been based on copying Old Masters. This self-likeness, in pencil on paper, was executed in London,
during a visit to see his friend Whistler, through whom he learned to etch.
(Fitzwilliam Museum, University of Cambridge, England)

IGNACE HENRI JEAN FANTIN-LATOUR (1836–1904), 1883
This self-likeness of the French artist depicts the mature man, who now rejected modern life in favour of French art of
the previous century and classical music of the Romantic period as a source for his work.
The static image, subtly but expressively lit within a monochrome space, describes solitude and isolation.
(Galleria degli Uffizi, Florence, Italy)

IGNACE HENRI JEAN FANTIN-LATOUR (1836–1904), 1864
The French artist exhibited this painting, *Homage to Delacroix*, at the Salon of 1864, as a tribute to the great artist who had recently died. It includes the painters Legros and Whistler, behind and in front of his own seated figure, Manet and the novelist Baudelaire. Among his avant-garde friends, who shared his taste for recording modern life, the artist is distinctive in his working shirt and with his palette on his knee. Having rejected the anecdotal character of contemporary figure groups, Fantin-Latour's picture is strongly individual in form.
(Musée d'Orsay, Paris France)

GIOVANNI FATTORI (1825–1908), 1854
The Italian painter and etcher started his career painting military subjects, but later he turned to landscapes
and became one of the leading *plein-air* painters in Italy, living and working in Florence.
(Galleria d'Arte Moderna, Florence, Italy)

JOHN DUNCAN FERGUSSON (1874–1961), C. 1902
Fergusson, a self-taught Scottish artist who abandoned a career in medicine to devote himself to painting,
began by making impressionistic sketches of his family and of Edinburgh. The style of the self-portrait,
with its strong lines and compositional simplicity, was one that he was to develop further.
(Scottish National Portrait Gallery, Edinburgh, Scotland/The Fergusson Gallery, Perth and Kinross Council, Scotland)

GIOVANNI DOMENICO FERRETTI (1692–1769), 1719
The Italian artist was schooled in academic traditions and achieved considerable success in his native Florence.
He decorated the interiors of the city's private palaces and churches with mythological and religious frescoes,
and received official honours and positions. He is known also for a series of 'Harlequinades',
illustrating scenes from the *Commedia dell'Arte*.
(Galleria degli Uffizi, Florence, Italy)

ANSELM FEUERBACH (1829–1880), c. 1860
Feuerbach was keen to break away from the rigid and pedantic art of his home country, Germany, and in this
self-portrait draws upon the style of the Old Masters. The artist is clearly working on a painting,
and he looks as if he has turned his profile momentarily towards the viewer.
(Hermitage, St Petersburg, Russia)

LAVINIA FONTANA (c. 1552–1614), c. 1595
Lavinia was the daughter of the painter Prospero Fontana (1512–97), who worked as an assistant to Vasari.
The portrait of Lavinia who, after Sofonisba Anguissola, was the most successful woman artist
in Florence, was painted by herself, or possibly by her father.
(Galleria degli Uffizi, Florence, Italy)

FOUJITA (1886–1968), 1926
Foujita, a French painter of Japanese birth, made a number of similar self-portraits. He depicted himself working on a
sketch or a painting and often included a cat, which, with his idiosyncratic hairstyle, became a trademark.
The delicacy of his line, on a pale background as here, won him much admiration in France.
(Phillips, The International Fine Art Auctioneers, London, England/©ADAGP, Paris and DACS, London 1999)

JEAN FOUQUET (c.1415–81), c. 1440
The self-portrait medallion by one of the leading painters of the Renaissance in France is only
2¾ inches (7 cm) in diameter; much of Fouquet's work was done as an illuminator.
The gold is painted on a dark background of enamel over a copper base.
(Musée du Louvre, Paris, France)

JEAN-HONORÉ FRAGONARD (1732–1806), c, 1760
Fragonard was perhaps the most brilliant and versatile artist of eighteenth-century France. A champion
of the Rococo, he reacted against the formality of the old-fashioned court of Louis XIV
and focused on all that was charming and elegant, as shown by this self-portrait.
(Museée Fragonard, Grasse, France)

ROBERT FRANKLAND-RUSSELL (1784–1849), c. 1824
The English painter here portrays himself on horseback, jumping a fence in the winter countryside.
Frankland-Russell's principal subject-matter was horses and hounds, and the English landscape.
(Chequers, Buckinghamshire, England)

GIOVANNA FRATELLINI (1666–1731), 1720
The Florentine has portrayed herself casting a glance over her shoulder as she works at her easel. The miniature is said
to be of her son Lorenzo, who was also a painter, and she is perhaps indicating that she belongs to a family of artists.
(Galleria degli Uffizi, Florence, Italy)

LUCIAN FREUD (born 1922), 1943
This was painted when the English artist Lucian Freud was only twenty-one. At that time he was particularly
interested in sketching faces, and here uses himself as a model. The lines are crisply drawn, the face
exaggerated with bulbous eyes, and colour subtly picked out in crayon.
(Private Collection)

LUCIAN FREUD (born 1922), 1949
One of the English artist's earlier works, this is essentially a facial study. Freud experiments here with form and paint
technique, and depicts himself as an ordinary man rather than making a statement about the role of the artist.
(Private Collection)

LUCIAN FREUD (born 1922), 1963
The English artist is well known for his portraits emphasizing realistic physical form, and here he uses himself as
model. Freud rests his head on his hand, perhaps looking down into a mirror, and builds up bone structure
and skin with bold, thick brushstrokes. The neutral tones convey a somewhat haggard appearance.
(Whitworth Art Gallery, Manchester, England)

LUCIAN FREUD (born 1922), 1967
Freud catches a glimpse of himself in a hand mirror in this interesting self-portrait.
The mirror stands on the cross-bar of a slightly raised sash window,
and the artist places emphasis upon his own rather blurred image by leaving the view outside unpainted.
(Private Collection)

den 8ᵗᵉ März 1802

CASPAR DAVID FRIEDRICH (1774–1840), 1802
The pencil and wash study is probably from the German artist's sketchbook. It shows him in informal pose,
wearing an eyeshade and with a water-bottle for his painting fastened to a buttonhole.
(Kunsthalle, Leipzig, Germany)

CASPAR DAVID FRIEDRICH (1774–1840), 1818–19
The oil painting, entitled *The White Cliffs of Rugen*, includes the cloaked figure of the master of Romanticism
on the right. With his back turned, it is as if he is sharing with the spectator the wonders of the view
opened up between the cliffs and over the water.
(Oskar Reinhart Collection, Winterthur, Switzerland)

CASPAR DAVID FRIEDRICH (1774–1840), c. 1835
Each of the five ships corresponds to a figure on the
shore. The old man facing towards the sunset,
characteristically with his back turned, is a portrait of
the artist, symbolically confronting his own decline:
the title of this picture is *The Stages of Life*.
The children are probably his son and daughter.
Friedrich wrote, 'The artist should not only paint what
he sees before him, but also what he sees within him'.
(Museum der Künste, Leipzig, Germany)

HENRY FUSELI (1741–1825), c. 1780
As the most imaginative and original history painter of his generation, who drew his subjects from Shakespeare and
Milton, this Swiss-born English artist believed that the use of the poetic image in painting defined human experience.
This self-likeness, in black chalk, reflects the intensity of his presence noted by contemporaries.
(Private Collection)

THOMAS GAINSBOROUGH (1727–88), C. 1738–39
The portrait of himself, in oil on panel, was painted by Gainsborough at the age of eleven or twelve, while he was still
living at home at Sudbury in Suffolk. It is therefore the work of a child. A few years later he went to London
to study under the French draughtsman and engraver Gravelot.
(Private Collection)

THOMAS GAINSBOROUGH (1727–88), 1746
Painted in the year of his marriage to Margaret Burr, Gainsborough was by now living in London and had set up his own studio. Seated on a bench in parkland, the painter depicts himself as having laid aside a book and motioning to his wife with his hand. In the background is a classical temple, perhaps symbolizing the Temple of Hymen.
(Musée du Louvre, Paris, France)

THOMAS GAINSBOROUGH (1727–88), c. 1749
Returned to his native Suffolk, Gainsborough painted a portrait of himself with his wife and daughter Mary,
who was born in 1748. He was a devoted husband and an affectionate father to his two daughters.
Impulsive by nature, he was fun-loving and his conversation was described as 'sprightly, but licentious'.
(Private Collection)

THOMAS GAINSBOROUGH (1727–88), 1754
This is a portrait of the artist in his mid-twenties, a sketch in which only the head and tricorne hat were completed.
He shows himself with a rather quizzical expression, searching for the 'peculiarity of countenance' that he was
constantly observing. He believed that likeness was 'the principal beauty and intention of a Portrait'.
(Private Collection)

THOMAS GAINSBOROUGH (1727–88), C. 1787
Painted for his friend Abel, this was the portrait of himself by which he wished to be remembered.
He gave his consent that after his death an engraving could be made of the sketch.
The picture was given to the Royal Academy by his younger daughter Margaret.
(Royal Academy of Arts, London, England)

PAUL GAUGUIN (1848–90), 1889–90
In the background of Gauguin's self-portrait is his painting *The Yellow Christ*, inspired by a carved wooden Crucifix
in the church of Trémolo, near Pont Aven. The picture is shown in reverse, as he would have seen it in a mirror.
At Pont-Aven in Brittany the French painter developed the Post-Impressionist style described as 'Synthesism'.
(Private Collection)

PAUL GAUGUIN (1848–90), 1893
The French artist, whose quest for a simpler way of living and a more potent experience of life took him to Tahiti,
painted this portrait of himself as his travels were coming to an end. The crudity of the technique was his
attempt to imitate the primitive, unspoiled character of Polynesian culture.
(Norton Simon Collection, Pasadena, USA)

PAUL GAUGUIN (1848–90), 1893–94
The cool colours indicate a different direction in Gauguin's work. In the background is one of his pictures
painted in Tahiti, and it is as if he had literally put that phase in his artistic development behind him,
reflecting on its significance to him rather than expressing it directly.
(Musée d'Orsay, Paris, France)

PAUL GAUGUIN (1848–90), 1896
The title of the picture is *Self-portrait, Close to Golgotha*. The picture was painted at a time when Gauguin
was suffering deeply from his rejection by artists in Paris, and from ill-health and bouts of depression. The expression
on his face is tortured. Two dark figures lurk in the background, the one on the left perhaps a small Death-head.
(Museu de Arte, São Paulo, Brazil)

RICHARD GERSTL (1883–1908), 1908
The startling image of the Austrian was painted in the year of his suicide. His paintings were never exhibited during his
lifetime, and he was able to exist as a painter with financial help from his father. Here, the vitality of the brush marks
and the strong source of light, illuminating the face from below, make this a work of great intensity.
(Österreichische Galerie, Vienna, Austria)

MARK GERTLER (1891–1939), c. 1910
The English painter here combined a reflection of himself in a convex mirror with a still-life that includes
a Japanese figure. Gertler, the son of Polish Jews, was able to pursue an artistic career as a young man through
financial assistance from the Jewish Educational Aid Society. He went as a student to the Slade school of art,
where he met, and fell in love with, the painter Dora Carrington.
(City Art Gallery, Leeds Museums and Galleries, England/Courtesy of Luke Gertler)

DOMENICO GHIRLANDAIO (1449–94), 1485

This is the altarpiece of the church of Santa Trinità in Florence, depicting the Adoration of the Shepherds.
Ghirlandaio, who was admired for his religious narrative paintings, included a portrait of himself
as one of the shepherds on the right-hand side of the main scene.
With one hand he gestures to the Christ Child and with the other to his heart.
(Santa Trinità, Florence, Italy)

DETAIL
The expression on the face of the Italian artist, in the guise of a shepherd, expresses humility in the presence of Christ.
The angle of his head is as it would conveniently have been seen reflected in a mirror.

ERIC GILL (1882–1940), 1927
In a solemn and unconventional self-likeness, executed as a wood engraving, the English artist is wearing a version of
the stone-mason's traditional paper hat. His life in artistic communities, and work as a sculptor, printmaker,
letter-cutter and influential typographic designer, were closely bound up with religious, social and moral issues.
(Wolseley Fine Arts, London, England/Courtesy of Mrs Douglas Cleverdon)

LUCA GIORDANO (1634–1705), c. 1665
Among the patrons of this famous and successful Italian artist were the Medici, and the monarchs of Spain and France.
His vast output, in a powerful Spanish-influenced Baroque style for religious works, and a more elegant, lighter-
coloured classicism, included altarpieces, landscapes, portraits, and decorative fresco cycles.
(Galleria degli Uffizi, Florence, Italy)

VINCENT VAN GOGH (1853–90), 1886
This prodigiously productive Dutchman was active as an artist for only ten years. He was largely self-taught and
wanted initially to be a painter of working people, rapidly developing his skills and distinctive style through a series of
self-portraits. This sombre self-likeness was done in the year he arrived in Paris.
(Haags Gemeentemuseum, The Netherlands)

VINCENT VAN GOGH (1853–90), 1887
Responding to avant-garde developments in Paris, the Dutch artist learned fast. He began to experiment with colour,
by lightening his palette and using paint in a looser fashion to model form. Using the same image of himself
as in the previous picture, Van Gogh here experiments with sketchy and rhythmically rendered
oil paint in glowing colours on paper.
(Rijksmuseum Kröller-Müller, Otterlo, The Netherlands)

VINCENT VAN GOGH (1853–90), 1887
Introducing a straw hat into a much-worked self-image, Van Gogh was able, with a particularly expressive use of loose
brushstrokes, to explore the theory of complementary colours. He was experimenting with using a limited number of
colours in large areas. Painted on canvas, this painting was laid on panel.
(The Detroit Institute of Arts, USA, City of Detroit Purchase)

VINCENT VAN GOGH (1853–90), 1887–8
In another self-image and using a different contrast of colours, Van Gogh uses loose brushstrokes in tones
of blue for the background, The coat and hat reflect the texture of his red beard,
the colour of which he has heightened for contrasting effect.
(Rijksmuseum Vincent Van Gogh, Amsterdam, The Netherlands)

VINCENT VAN GOGH (1853–90), 1888
Having moved to Arles, where he hoped to establish a community of artists, the Dutch artist produced a self-portrait in
deference to the artistic theories of abstraction of his friend Paul Gauguin. He considered this unsigned self-image
a study. Its Oriental, flat areas of saturated colour are defined by heavy contour lines.
(Fogg Art Museum, Harvard University, Cambridge, USA, Bequest from the Collection of Maurice Wertheim, Class 1906)

VINCENT VAN GOGH (1853–90), 1888
The self-portrait of Van Gogh at his easel was done at the end of his time in Paris. Its unusual composition displays the
influence of cheap Japanese woodblock prints, which he and other avant-garde artists were collecting.
This is apparent in its simplicity, its more linear forms and flattened perspective.
(Rijksmuseum Vincent Van Gogh, Amsterdam, The Netherlands)

181

VINCENT VAN GOGH (1853–90), 1889
This was painted while Van Gogh was at Saint-Rémy, where he had institutionalized himself for a year. The use of flat greys, heightened only by the red of his hair and beard, contrasts with the intensity of emotional effect achieved by the Dutch artist through the movement created by the swirling paint.
(Musée d'Orsay, Paris, France)

VINCENT VAN GOGH (1853–90), 1889
Early in 1889 Van Gogh painted this famous self-likeness, after cutting off his ear and suffering his first attack
of mental illness. This was after the departure of Gauguin from Arles. The light of the south of France
infuses the colour of the long brushstrokes that do not differentiate between the varying textures
of his coat, the fur on his hat and the Japanese print on the wall behind.
(Courtauld Gallery, London, England)

VASILI (WILHELM-AUGUST) ALEKSANDROVICH GOLIKE (1802–48), 1834
The Russian artist Golike is the man standing on the right, with his two children in the foreground.
George Dawe is shown seated with pen in hand. The English artist, who died in 1829, had gone to Russia in 1819
at the invitation of Tsar Alexander I and stayed for nine years, painting nearly 400 portraits
of Russian officers from the Napoleonic Wars and the Imperial family.
(State Russian Museum, St Petersburg, Russia)

ALEKSANDR YAKOVLEVICH GOLOVIN (1863–1930), 1927
Known primarily as a designer for the stage, this Russian artist worked for the Imperial theatre in St Petersburg
and for Diaghilev's first productions in Paris. His portraits combine subtle psychological insight with an
interest in the decorative qualities of Oriental art. He painted in tempera on canvas.
(Private Collection)

HENDRIK GOLTZIUS (1558–1617), 1604
The large-scale pen and brown ink drawing on canvas of Bacchus, Venus and Ceres illustrates the virtuosity
and technical brilliance of the Dutch artist, whose engravings were widely circulated at the time.
(Hermitage, St Petersburg, Russia)

DETAIL
Goltzius has inserted into the composition an image of himself at an altar, a rather incongruous witness to the scene.

FRANCISCO JOSÉ DE GOYA Y LUCIENTES (1746–1828),
1800. The focus of this large-scale, official family
portrait of the Spanish king, Charles IV, and his family
is the powerful Queen Maria Luisa. By contrast, the
Spanish artist, who served three generations of
Bourbon royalty, has positioned himself on the left,
in shadow, and in front of a large easel.
(Prado, Madrid, Spain)

FRANCISCO JOSÉ DE GOYA Y LUCIENTES (1746–1828), c. 1800
Over six decades of artistic activity the Spanish artist, as observer and witness, sensitively and incisively recorded
the political and social turmoil of his time in many paintings, prints and drawings.
Despite the official suppression of some of his prints, he was known abroad as the 'Apelles of Spain'.
(Musée Bonnat, Bayonne, France)

FRANCISCO JOSÉ DE GOYA Y LUCIENTES (1746–1828), c.1790–95
This self-likeness, in a new small format, was painted during his recovery from an illness which damaged the hearing of
the Spanish artist. The flamboyant image, dramatically lit from the window, reveals the hyperactive energy
with which he was working, with final effects added by the light of candles fixed to his hat.
(Academia de San Fernando, Madrid, Spain)

BENOZZO GOZZOLI (1420–97), 1459
Around three of the walls of the chapel of Piero de' Medici's Florentine palace, Gozzoli painted the procession of the
Three Magi. Figures in the fresco include portraits of the Medici family and their household.
(Palazzo Medici-Riccardi, Florence, Italy)

DETAIL

Among the faces in the crowd following the procession is Benozzo Gozzoli's self-portrait. He is conspicuous for the gold lettering on his red cap, which reads 'OPVUS BENOTTII D'.

EL GRECO [DOMENICO THEOTOCOPULI] (1541–1614), 1580–85
The subject of the painting by the Spanish artist is the Holy Family with St Elizabeth and the child
St John the Baptist. El Greco was born in Crete (hence his name), studied in Venice,
worked in Venice and Rome, and from 1577 lived in Toledo in Spain.
(Museo de Santa Cruz, Toledo, Spain)

DETAIL
The figure of the painter appears in a more distant plane to that of the Holy Family, his expression and the direction of his eyes more involving of the spectator than of the other participants in the scene.

EL GRECO [DOMENICO THEOTOCOPULI] (1541–1614), 1586–88
The subject of *The Burial of Count Orgaz* is based on a legend of 1323. The cold, bluish range of colours of his
paintings done in Spain replaced the richer ones influenced by his stay in Venice.
Here, El Greco created a contrast between the naturalism of the dark-clad figures that were portraits of
contemporary people and the extravagant handling of the celestial apparition above.
(S. Tomé, Toledo, Spain)

DETAIL

The long, thin head of El Greco, as a witness to the miracle, is the seventh from the left.
He received unanimous acclaim from his contemporaries as a portraitist.

EL GRECO [DOMENICO THEOTOCOPULI] (1541–1614), 1612–14
This is the altarpiece of Santo Domingo el Antiguo, depicting the Adoration of the Shepherds. The artist has included a
likeness of himself as the second figure from the right, his hands raised in worship. With the luminescence radiating
from the Infant Christ, El Greco endowed the nocturnal scene with dramatic radiance.
(Prado, Madrid, Spain)

EDWARD JOHN GREGORY (1850–1909), 1887
Gregory started work in the drawing office of the P & O Steamship Company but soon decided to become an artist
full time. He spent years working on his masterpiece, *Boulter's Lock: Sunday Afternoon*, which depicts Londoners
boating on the Thames. After it was exhibited at the Royal Academy in 1898 he was elected a Royal Academician
and began a fruitful career as a portrait-painter. Here he has painted himself in Elizabethan dress.
(Chris Beetles Ltd, London, England)

JEAN-BAPTISTE GREUZE (1725–1805), 1785
The French painter gained fame when his picture *Father of the Family Reading the Bible* was shown at the
Paris Salon in 1755. He specialized in genre paintings with a moral tale to tell, and these were widely known
in the form of engravings. His genre paintings are today less admired than his portraits.
(Musée du Louvre, Paris, France)

GEORGE GROSZ (1893–1959), 1938
In the painting *Self-portrait, Admonishing*, the German-American has portrayed himself making the
sign of the Benediction. After his years as a caricaturist and leading member of the Dada group in Berlin,
Grosz, in collar and tie, seems the image of respectability.
(Galerie Nierendorf, Berlin, Germany/© DACS 1999)

JOHANNES GUMPP (born 1626), 1646
This is a triple image of the Austrian artist. He has portrayed himself from behind, with the reflection
of his face in a mirror that he is copying in a painting. His own view of the mirror-image as it is
emerging on the easel is subtly different from that of the viewer of the picture.
(Galleria degli Uffizi, Florence, Italy)

CORNELIUS NORBERTUS GYSBRECHTS (1659–72), c. 1670
The distinctive work of this obscure Flemish artist, who worked in Germany and Denmark, consist of illusionistic and ornamental *Vanitas* still-lifes, reminding the spectator of the transience and uncertainty of life. This was an art form peculiar to northern Europe. The personalized collection of letters, a violin, an artist's easel and a miniature self-portrait create an allegorical self-image, showing the worldly goods that defined his life.
(Royal Castle, Warsaw, Poland)

MARIA-CHRISTINA HABSBURG, ARCHDUCHESS OF AUSTRIA (1742–98), 1776
This was the work of a talented amateur artist with an eye for detail. The archduchess chose to portray herself
at a spinning-wheel, surrounded by the fine objects and furniture of her private apartments.
(Kunsthistorisches Museum, Vienna, Austria)

FRANCESCO HAYEZ (1791–1881), 1860
Hayez lived through a turbulent period in his native Italy and became associated with the political struggle
through his patriotic paintings of romantic scenes from Italian literature, history and opera.
He has adopted the pose of a statesman or soldier, displaying the weapons used by the artist.
(Galleria degli Uffizi, Florence, Italy)

GEORGE HAYTER (1792–1871), c. 1840
Sir George Hayter was never accepted in official art circles in England because of his unconventional private life,
but he achieved success for a time as the young Queen Victoria's royal image-maker.
This is the role in which he cast himself, looking towards the viewer as the subject of his painting.
(Private Collection)

JOHN HAZLITT (1767–1837), 1802
Brother of the English essayist William Hazlitt, John worked primarily as a miniaturist, though he did paint
some larger portraits. This one of himself was done in watercolour on ivory and measures 41 x 33 inches (105 x 85 cm).
As an artist he was self-taught, enjoying some success with his brother's literary friends, Coleridge among them.
(Maidstone Museum and Art Gallery, England)

MAARTEN VAN HEEMSKERK (1498–1574), 1553
This is a double self-portrait, the picture containing a reference to the Netherlandish painter's earlier stay in Rome in the small seated figure making a drawing of the Colosseum that is in the background of the main portrait.
(Fitzwilliam Museum, University of Cambridge, England)

NICHOLAS HILLIARD (1547–1618), 1577
This youthful and refined image of the English miniaturist was painted when he was thirty. He has portrayed himself
in exquisite dress, more like the Elizabethan courtiers and gentlemen who commissioned his images
than the struggling working artist. It is painted on vellum and mounted on card.
(Victoria & Albert Museum, London, England)

WILLIAM HOGARTH (1697–1764), c. 1735–40
In this, his earliest known portrait, Hogarth scrutinizes his face in a mirror. The English painter,
printmaker and art theorist campaigned to raise the status of artists and ensure their financial independence
from aristocratic patronage through legal possession of the copyright for prints made from their paintings.
(Yale Center for British Art, Paul Mellon Collection, USA)

EDWARD HOPPER (1882–1967), c. 1925–30
The American artist created an influential and enduring vision of his native country. The sense of empty space and the
distinctive lighting in his paintings of rural landscapes and figures in urban settings express a stillness that appears
isolated and detached. The gaze of his self-likeness seems to require no response.
(Whitney Museum of American Art, New York, USA)

WILLIAM HENRY HUNT (1790–1864), c. 1830–40
Hunt was an English watercolourist who specialized in humorous and sentimental figure subjects in rustic settings.
His prominent forehead and striking eyes were noted by contemporaries. In the 1830s he began
to stipple his colour, as here, over a ground of gummed white.
(Blackburn Museum and Art Gallery, England)

WILLIAM HOLMAN HUNT (1827–1910), 1845
Hunt painted this confident self-portrait, rich in brown tones, a year after he joined the Royal Academy Schools.
It was at that time that the English artist met John Everett Millais, with whom, together with
Dante Gabriel Rossetti, he founded the Pre-Raphaelite Brotherhood in 1848. This work demonstrates the intensely
observed realism that was to be central to the Pre-Raphaelites' aims.
(Birmingham Museums and Art Gallery, England)

JEAN AUGUSTE DOMINIQUE INGRES (1780–1867), 1804
An artist committed to the classical tradition, and the father of academicism, the French painter here portrays himself
at the age of twenty-four, when he was rapidly becoming one of the leading portrait-painters of his time.
(Musée Condé, Chantilly, France)

JEAN AUGUSTE DOMINIQUE INGRES (1780–1867), 1858
Ingres sent this dignified self-portrait wearing the red badge of the *légion d'honneur* to the Uffizi in 1858.
He deliberately chose to portray himself in modest attire 'so that the great painters in whose company
I shall sit cannot accuse me of a prideful temerity'.
(Galleria degli Uffizi, Florence, Italy)

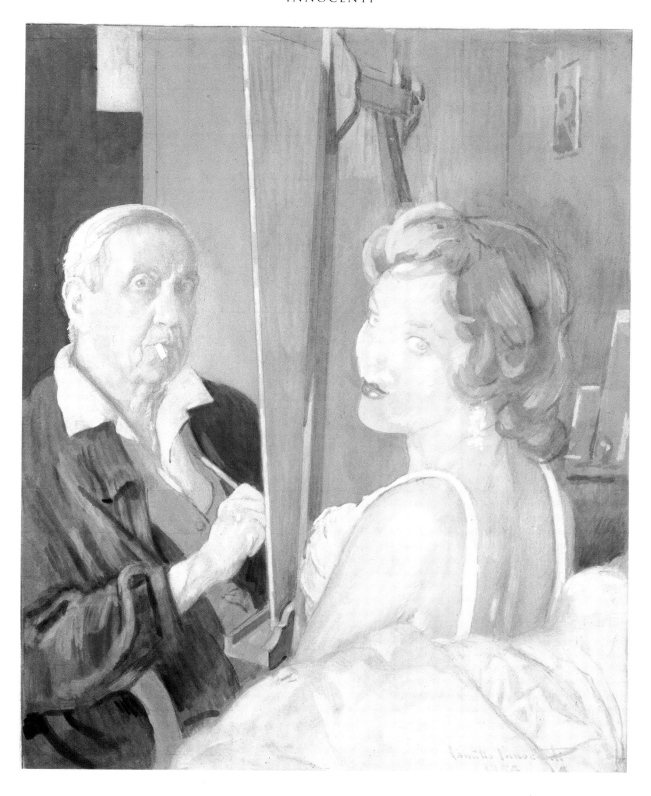

CAMILLO INNOCENTI (1871–1961), c. 1951
Here the Italian artist portrays himself at his easel, at work on this double portrait of himself and his model.
The treatment of the female figure seems more stylized than that of Innocenti:
the woman is slightly idealized whereas he has indicated the truth about his own age.
Women attending to their dress and hair was one of the artist's main subjects.
(Bonhams, London, England)

JEAN-BAPTISTE ISABEY (1767–1855), c. 1800–5
This self-portrait is a miniature, in enamel on ivory. The French painter developed a sentimental style of portraiture
that was popular with his mainly aristocratic clientele. It perfectly exemplifies the Romantic spirit of the age.
(Wallace Collection, London, England)

AUGUSTUS JOHN (1878–1961), 1956
Famous for his bohemian lifestyle, this gifted English artist was adopted as a favourite society portrait-painter.
His extravagant personality is clearly seen in this lithographic self-likeness. The best-known of his works
are of his large and unconventional family, and of the landscapes encountered
during the periods they spent travelling in a gypsy caravan.
(Private Collection/© Bridgeman Art Library, London/Julius White)

DOROTHY JOHNSTONE (1892–1980), 1923
In the Scottish artist's *Rest Time in the Life Class* the students discuss their drawings as the model relaxes. Johnstone
has included herself in the top right-hand corner of the picture. She was a teacher at the Edinburgh College of Art,
where she had completed her own training, and portrayed herself here in that role.
(City of Edinburgh Museums and Art Galleries, Scotland/Courtesy of Dr DA Sutherland & Lady JE Sutherland)

JACOB JORDAENS (1593–78), c. 1621–22
The artist holds a lute in this painting of himself with his wife Catharina, his mischievous daughter Elizabeth
and a servant. The painting, as well as representing the Flemish painter's family, can be interpreted
as an allegory of love, fidelity and the bounty of marriage.
(Prado, Madrid, Spain)

ANGELICA KAUFFMANN (1741–1807), 1787
Born in Switzerland, Angelica became famous in England and Italy for her decorative paintings.
She did several self-portraits, each giving the impression that she was a woman of gentle modesty.
(Galleria degli Uffizi, Florence, Italy)

SEAN KEATING (1889–1977), c. 1930
As a leading artist of the new Irish Free State, Keating painted the heroes of the nationalist cause,
the poet Yeats and de Valera. He favoured an idealized, heroic interpretation of Ireland and its people.
In this chalk drawing he pictures himself as a rugged working man.
(Taylor Gallery, London, England/Courtesy of Justin & Michael Keating)

WILLEM KEY (c. 1515–68), c. 1553
Key was one of a generation of Flemish artists whose Northern 'realism' gave way to the Italian 'idealism' and Venetian
colouring of this panel painting. His self-likeness, in the second figure from the right at the back of the main group,
looks out towards the viewer and is detached from the emotional intensity of the scene before him.
(Phillips, The International Fine Art Auctioneers, London, England)

ERNST LUDWIG KIRCHNER (1880–1938), 1905
The energetic German painter, printmaker and sculptor has created a self-image with a nude model. His paintings of small figure groups in urban settings done just before the First World War express the nervous agitation of the time.
(Private Collection/Copyright by Dr Wolfgang & Ingeborg Henze-Ketterer, Wichtrach/Bern)

BORIS MIKHAILOVICH KUSTODIEV (1878–1927), 1910
The Russian painter, born in Astrakhan, has portrayed himself in a luxurious interior, his face lit from the right from an
unseen window. The vivid blues in the background were often to be found in Kustodiev's work as he liked to use the
intense colours of Russian folk art, especially when he was painting the merchant class in a satirical manner.
He saw his palette as having also an Oriental richness, relating to his Astrakhan heritage.
(Pushkin Museum, Moscow, Russia)

NICOLAS DE LARGILLIÈRE (1656–1746), c. 1695
The French artist was one of the most successful portrait-painters of the second half of Louis XIV's reign.
He was extremely prolific and by the end of his career had produced some 1,500 portraits.
(Rafael Valls Gallery, London, England)

CARL LARSSON (1853–1919), 1900
Larsson is best known for his influence on interior design through his reinterpretation of Swedish folk art and culture.
He produced numerous self-portraits, most of which show him as happy and self-consciously mischievous.
This one has the title *In Front of the Mirror*.
(Göteborgs Kunstmuseum, Sweden)

MARIE LAURENCIN (1883–1956), 1924
The French painter worked also as a stage designer and illustrator. With its soft pink, blue and grey tones, and the blackness of the eyes, this self-portrait is an example of Laurencin's mature style that developed after she had taken refuge in Spain during the First World War. It was a style that won her much popularity as a society portrait-painter when she returned to Paris in 1923, a year before this picture was painted.
(Galerie Daniel Malingue, Paris, France/© ADAGP, Paris and DACS, London 1999)

THOMAS LAWRENCE (1769–1830), 1810

This portrait of Lawrence by himself was executed in chalk and watercolour on paper. His work epitomized the Regency style in England and appealed to the Prince Regent, who commissioned the artist to paint all the men who took part in the defeat of Napoleon. This became the series of portraits in the Waterloo Chamber at Windsor Castle.

(Ashmolean Museum, Oxford, England)

THOMAS LAWRENCE (1769–1830), 1787–88
A child genius, Lawrence was made an Associate of the Royal Academy in 1791 at the age of twenty-two,
a Royal Academician in 1794 and President of the Royal Academy in 1820.
In 1792 he was appointed Painter in Ordinary to the King, in succession to Reynolds.
(Berger Collection, Denver, USA)

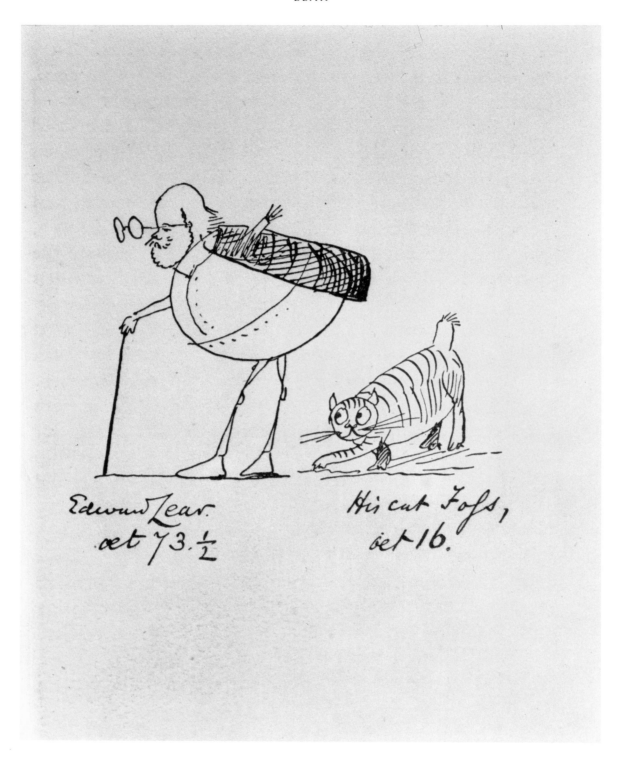

EDWARD LEAR (1812–88), 1885
The well-loved English composer of Limericks and nonsense stories often illustrated letters to his friends and patrons with drawings of himself and his cat-without-a-tail, Foss. The plainness of Lear's face was emphasized by his shortsightedness; his style of dress was described as 'careless by courtesy'.
(*Later Letters of Edward Lear*, edited by Lady Strachey, 1911)

CHARLES LE BRUN (1619–90), 1683–84
As the *Premier Peintre du Roi* to Louis XIV, the French artist supervised every detail of the new royal palace of Versailles — its architecture, furnishings and landscape — and executed its decoration. He also managed the royal collection of paintings and drawings, and designed for the Gobelins, the royal tapestry manufactory.
(Galleria degli Uffizi, Florence, Italy)

ALPHONSE LEGROS (1837–1911), 1858
Born in France, Legros spent much of his life in England, working as an etcher, painter, sculptor and teacher.
It was Whistler who encouraged him to move to London in 1863. In 1876 he was recommended for the post of Professor
of Fine Art at the Slade School, where he continued until 1892. The self-portrait was executed in pen and ink on paper.
(Fitzwilliam Museum, Cambridge, England)

FREDERIC LEIGHTON (1830–96), 1880
The English Lord Leighton told a colleague, 'I am finishing my portrait for the Uffizi Gallery in the red cloak of a
Doctor of Oxford University, with the gold medal of a President of the Royal Academy hanging down.
It is like, very like!'
(Galleria degli Uffizi, Florence, Italy)

BERNARD LENS (1681–1740), 1724
Lens pictured himself here as a miniaturist, the format appropriately being a miniature. It was executed in gouache on
paper. The Englishman's work was strongly influenced by the Venetian artist Rosalba Carriera.
(Ashmolean Museum, Oxford, England)

LEONARDO DA VINCI (1452–1519), c .1513
Although his finished artistic output was small, this Italian painter, sculptor, architect, theorist, engineer and scientist
created the most famous painting in the world in the *Mona Lisa*, and his influence radically transformed European art.
This red chalk drawing is said to be a self-likeness of the man who appeared to represent universal genius.
(Biblioteca Reale, Turin, Italy)

PERCY WYNDHAM LEWIS (1882–1957), c. 1921–22
The sharp, decisive lines and planes of this self-portrait by the English painter and writer combine the angular
abstractions of Vorticism (the movement invented by Wyndham Lewis) and a more representational style.
The picture is called *Mr Wyndham Lewis as a Tyro*; Tyros were a fictional creation by the artist,
a breed of idiotic, grinning creatures that he wrote about in 1921–22 in the magazine *The Tyro*.
(Ferens Art Gallery, Hull City Museums and Art Galleries, England/Estate of Mrs GA Wyndham Lewis)

LIMBOURG BROTHERS (fl. c. 1405–15), c. 1415
Among the courtiers in this richly ornate miniature representing January are said to be self-likenesses of the three
brothers, Paul, Jean and Herman de Limbourg. They were the Flemish illuminators responsible for the illustrations in
the Book of Hours known as *Les Très Riches Heures du Duc de Berry*.
The Duke himself is seated at the centre of his table.
(Musée Condé, Chantilly, France)

JOHANNES LINGELBACH (1622–74), 1650
The German painter was active in The Netherlands and in Italy. This is an intriguing portrait:
the artist has painted himself sitting in front of his easel playing the violin, looking like a marionette,
while a studio assistant busies himself in the background.
(Johnny van Haeften Gallery, London, England)

J. E. Liotard
de Geneve Surnommé
le Peintre Turc peint
par lui meme à
Vienne 1744

JEAN-ETIENNE LIOTARD (1702–89), 1744
The Swiss artist here exhibits the clarity of his portrait style as well as his customarily eccentric appearance.
After living in Constantinople he adopted Turkish dress and was known as 'the Turkish painter',
contributing significantly to his celebrity in Europe.
(Galleria degli Uffizi, Florence, Italy)

JEAN-ETIENNE LIOTARD (1702–89), c. 1770–73
Liotard painted likenesses of himself both as exercises in self-examination and to advertise his skill as a
portrait-painter: such curiosities as this brought him to the notice of patrons and the public.
(Musée d'Art et d'Histoire, Geneva, Switzerland)

FILIPPINO LIPPI (c. 1457–1504), c. 1485
The unfinished self-portrait by the Florentine artist attests to his reputation as a fine draughtsman.
As a young man he was trained by his father, Fra Filippo Lippi, and by Botticelli.
The concentration on the features of the face suggest that this work was done as a study for a painting.
(Galleria degli Uffizi, Florence, Italy)

FILIPPINO LIPPI (c. 1457–1504), c. 1480
The Dispute with Simon Mago and the Crucifixion of St Peter is part of the cycle of frescoes in the Brancacci Chapel
in the Florentine church of Santa Maria del Carmine. Filippino was involved in other work in the chapel,
completing the fresco by Masaccio in which a self-portrait of that artist appears.
(Brancacci Chapel, Santa Maria del Carmine, Florence, Italy)

DETAIL
The head of a man on the far right of the painting is said to be modelled on Filippino, and painted by himself.

Anna Dorothea (Therbusch) Lisiewska (1721–82), c. 1776–77
Of Polish descent, this German artist was taught by her father to paint elegant portraits. Her work included
many self-portraits, this one done when she was of a certain age and having to use an eyeglass to read.
Many of her commissions were done for the Prussian court and Berlin society.
(Bode-Museum, Berlin, Germany)

GIOVANNI PAOLO LOMAZZO (1538–1600), C. 1570
Better known in intellectual circles as a metaphysical theorist on artistic creation,
this Italian artist gave up painting after 1571, when he began to go blind. He has painted himself as
the 'Abbot of the Academiglia', a pseudo-intellectual society that gave itself over to social pleasures.
(Pinacoteca di Brera, Milan, Italy)

LAMBERT LOMBARD (1506–66), c. 1550–60
This Flemish artist visited Rome in 1537 and modelled himself on the artists of Renaissance Italy; he was also an architect, humanist and collector of antique coins and medals. He believed that humanist learning should be part of the artist's training, and he founded the first academy in the Low Countries.
(Hermitage, St Petersburg, Russia)

KAZIMIR SEVERINOVICH MALEVICH (1878–1935), 1933
This Russian painter, printmaker and art theorist was a leading figure in avant-garde movements and a pioneer of Abstract art during the revolutionary periods before 1920. This decorative and unusually figurative self-portrait was done, with a pendant of his wife, at a time when his work was suppressed in Soviet Russia.
(State Russian Museum, St Petersburg, Russia)

EDOUARD MANET (1832–83), 1862
Twice a week crowds would gather in the Tuileries
gardens, attracted by the music. At the left-hand side of
the canvas is Manet himself with his studio companion
Albert de Balleroy. Baudelaire is the man on the left in a
group of three around the trunk of a tree, and to
Baudelaire's left is the bearded Fantin-Latour.
(National Gallery, London, England)

EDOUARD MANET (1832–83), 1879
Manet presents himself here in much the same role as in the previous picture, as a jaunty and elegant *boulevardier*.
The painter's atrributes of palette and paintbrush seem almost an afterthought, incidental to how he wished to be seen.
(Private Collection)

GIOVANNI MANNOZZI [DA SAN GIOVANNI] (1592–1636), c. 1620–25
The most individual artist among his Italian contemporaries, Mannozzi created bizarre and fanciful frescoes for the
palaces of cultivated patrons in Florence and Rome. His challenging, edgy gaze is tempered
by the sensuous use of paint and the facial mole that he has chosen to include.
(Galleria degli Uffizi, Florence, Italy)

ANDREA MANTEGNA (1431–1506), 1465–74
Appointed court painter to Lodovico Gonzaga, Marchese of Mantua, Mantegna carried out a series of frescoed
decorations for the ducal palace. The *Camera degli Sposi* has scenes from the life of the Gonzaga court,
remarkable for the illusion that the events are actually taking place, just above eye level.
(Palazzo Ducale, Mantua, Italy)

DETAIL

Well known for his subtlety and wit, Mantegna included a barely distinguishable likeness of himself among the foliage of the decoration of the illusionistically painted pilaster to the right of the doorway. The tablet above the door was once inscribed with a bold declaration that he was the painter of the work.

TOMMASO MASACCIO (1401–28), c. 1427
The Raising of the Son of Theophilus, the King of Antioch and St Peter Enthroned as First Bishop of Antioch
was finished c. 1480 by Filippino Lippi (1457/8–1504). The great fresco paintings of scenes from the life of St Peter were
done by Masaccio in the private chapel of the Brancacci family. He was acknowledged by contemporary Florentine
artists as the first painter to organize compositions using a linear system of perspective.
(Brancacci Chapel, Santa Maria del Carmine, Florence, Italy)

DETAIL

On the far right-hand side of the crowd Masaccio has pictured himself at the centre of the group, with Masolino (far left), his artistic collaborator on the frescoes of the chapel, Alberti (right), the author of *Della Pittura* (1436), who acknowledged Masaccio's artistic impact on the Renaissance of ancient art in Florence, and Brunelleschi (far right), the city's famed architect.

HENRI MATISSE (1869–1954), 1918
One of the great masters of twentieth-century art portrays himself in middle age, in suit and tie, sitting at his easel.
He is, of course, at work on the self-portrait that is this picture, as shown in a contemporary photograph;
the observer might be deluded, however, into thinking that the artist and the sitter had separate identities.
(Musée Matisse, Le Cateau-Cambrésis, France/Succession H Matisse/DACS 1999)

PAOLO MATTEIS (1662–1728), c. 1710
The painting is entitled *An Allegory of Painting, with a Self-Portrait of the Artist*. It shows a woman, personifying
Painting, putting the finishing touches to a portrait of the Italian artist Matteis. It has all the elegance and grace of style
for which Matteis was famous. He was particularly fond of the 'picture within a picture' theme and used it in a similar
way in his *Allegory of the Consequences of the Peace of Utrecht*.
(Private Collection)

ANTON MAUVE (1838–88), c. 1884/5
Mauve is one of the most admired painters of the Hague School. This self-portrait shows the Dutch artist in his studio
looking confidently towards the viewer. Some of the artist's landcape and animal pieces can be picked out
among the paintings that hang on the wall behind him.
(Haags Gemeentemuseum, The Netherlands)

LUIS EGIDIO MELÉNDEZ (1716–80), 1746
By the age of thirty, when he painted the portrait, the Spaniard's stance suggests confidence in his artistic abilities.
Though he presents a drawing of a male nude to the viewer, and holds the crayon with which he has been working,
Meléndez was best known as a painter of still-lifes.
(Musée du Louvre, Paris, France)

ANTON RAPHAEL MENGS (1728–79), c. 1773–74
This dynamic work was painted by the German artist and writer during his stay in Italy, a visit that lasted five years.
He depicted himself at work, looking intently at some unseen object, his brush and sketchpad in hand.
By comparison with other portraits of the time, Mengs's are unconventionally informal.
(Hermitage, St Petersburg, Russia)

GABRIEL METSU (1629–69), c. 1665
Like other of his Dutch contemporaries, Metsu is known for his interiors with figures, and informal portraits.
He spent the last twelve years of his life in Amsterdam, where he began to use cooler, greyer colours.
He has pictured himself here as a comfortable burgher, a character from one of his pictures.
(Johnny Van Haeften Gallery, London, England)

MICHELANGELO BURONARROTI (1475–1564), c. 1512
Although he was deeply concerned with the role and nature of the artist, this most celebrated Italian painter,
sculptor and architect of the High Renaissance never created a formal self-portrait.
A reference to himself appears in this painting of *The Last Judgement*.
(Vatican Museums and Galleries, Vatican City, Italy)

DETAIL

At the bottom right-hand corner of this detail of the fresco, on the end wall of the Sistine Chapel, the
flayed skin of St Bartholomew is a caricature image of the artist.

Tᴏᴍᴍᴀsᴏ Mɪɴᴀʀᴅɪ (1787–1871), 1813
Minardi has cast himself as the Romantic young artist living in a cramped and crudely-furnished garret.
The skulls are suitable artistic props, reminders of the presence of death in life. This long-lived Italian artist achieved
success at the Accademia di S. Luca in Rome, where he taught for over forty years.
(Galleria degli Uffizi, Florence, Italy)

JOHN MINTON (1917–57), 1946
A celebrity of London's bohemia and a distinctive illustrator and graphic artist, the Englishman shows himself,
in this emotionally charged pencil drawing, in the same pose as in a drawing that he did five years earlier.
It is as though he was reassessing his persona as an artist.
(Private Collection/© Royal College of Art)

JOAN MIRÒ (1893–1983), 1919

The Spanish painter, sculptor and printmaker, who was to become one of the most influential Abstract painters of the twentieth century, rendered himself in a contained and meticulous manner. The stylized exactness of his face and the folds of his red shirt show the influence of Cubism. The self-portrait was the first of his works in this style.

(Museo Picasso, Barcelona, Spain/© ADAGP, Paris and DACS, London 1999)

PAULA MODERSOHN-BECKER (1876–1907), 1906–07
This self-portrait by the German artist was painted at the end of her life. The gentle look on her face,
and the lacy veil, flowing gown and corsage of roses, all contribute to an image of great feminity,
expressed in simplified forms and beautiful colouring.
(Haags Gemeentemuseum, The Netherlands)

AMEDEO MODIGLIANI (1884–1920), 1919
An Italian painter and sculptor, Modigliani was part of the bohemian artists' community in Montparnasse, Paris.
He was a major artist of his generation, producing remarkable portraits of friends, colleagues and lovers,
and working at a furious pace until his death from tuberculosis.
(Museo de Arte, São Paulo, Brazil)

PIET MONDRIAN (1872–1944), 1918
This is a rare self-likeness of the Dutch artist, widely recognized by 1924 as being at the forefront of the international avant-garde. His Abstract paintings composed of the basic elements of line and colour — one of which is shown in the background — for him represented the concept of beauty and expressed the universal, dynamic pulse of life.
(Haags Gemeentemuseum, The Netherlands/©1999 Mondrian/Holtzman Trust
c/c Beeldrecht, Amsterdam, Holland & DACS, London)

CLAUDE MONET (1840–1926), 1917
This is Monet's last surviving self-portrait. He gave it to Georges Clemenceau, the French statesman, whose purchase
of a property near Giverny, close to Monet's, led to a friendship between the two.
It was probably Clemenceau who was the inspiration for Monet's *Grandes Décorations de Nymphéas*,
the water-lily paintings for the Orangerie of the Tuileries.
(Musée d'Orsay, Paris, France)

ANTONIS MOR (1517–76), 1558
The picture was one of the first from a Netherlandish artist to show the painter in front of his own easel, with brushes,
mahlstick and palette. The Greek text attached to his canvas alludes to the painter's virtue.
(Galleria degli Uffizi, Florence, Italy)

JACOB MORE (1740–93), 1783
The elegant self-portrait of the Scottish artist sketching, his coat and hat laid aside, was painted in Rome,
according to the inscription, and presented to the Uffizi on a visit to Florence in 1784.
From the 1770s More worked mainly in Italy, as a designer as well as a painter of landscapes.
(Galleria degli Uffizi, Florence, Italy)

GEORGE MORLAND (1763–1804), c. 1800
Morland was popular in the late eighteenth century for his pictures of animals and the English rural scene,
many of which were engraved. This painting of the artist outside the Bell Inn combines the two types of subject
with that of portraiture. The original drawing for the picture was known to have been his favourite portrait of himself.
(Berger Collection, Denver, USA)

GIOVANNI BATTISTA MORONI (c. 1525–78), c. 1570
The Italian artist's self-likeness, as one of the apostles, is distinguishable by the direct gaze towards the spectator
of the figure on the left of this panel painting of the Assumption of the Virgin.
Known for his natural and simple portrayal of religious mysteries, his accomplished portraits,
with their engaging immediacy, were mainly of middle-class residents of his native Brescia.
(Pinacoteca di Brera, Milan, Italy)

BARTOLOMÉ ESTEBAN MURILLO (1617–82), 1670s
The inscription states that the Spaniard painted the portrait of himself for his children. His right hand reaching over the frame, belonging both to the picture within the frame and to a separate reality, is an ingenious illusionistic device.
(National Gallery, London, England)

ROBERT NANTEUIL (1623–78), c. 1660–65
This French artist was appointed royal portrait engraver to King Louis XIV. Most of his subjects were royalty,
courtiers and high-ranking members of Parisian society. He was extremely accomplished at working in pastel,
the medium he used to create his own informal image, appearing self-contained
and satisfied with his place in the world.
(Galleria degli Uffizi. Florence, Italy)

CHRISTOPHER RICHARD WYNNE NEVINSON (1889–1946), c. 1911
This work in silverpoint was done in the English painter's first year at the Slade school of art and attests to Nevinson's skill as a draughtsman. He later became affiliated with Futurism, a movement that celebrated the dynamism of the machine age, and moved away from traditional representations such as this self-portrait.
(Wolseley Fine Arts, London, England/© Courtesy of the Nevinson Estate/Bridgeman Art Library, London)

JAMES NORTHCOTE (1746–1831), 1823
The English painter, a pupil of Reynolds, did several portraits of his brother as a falconer in a similar pose.
While he portrays his brother in full mastery of the falcon, he shows himself approaching the bird with uncertainty.
(Royal Albert Memorial Museum, Exeter, England)

JAMES NORTHCOTE (1746–1831), c. 1825
The artist here paints himself at work on a portrait of the Scottish writer Sir Walter Scott. Scott described him
as 'the old wizzard Northcote. He really resembles an animated mummy.' The painter's cap was
a conscious reference to the one worn by Titian in old age.
(Royal Albert Memorial Museum, Exeter, England)

GIUSEPPE NUVOLONE (16191703), c. 1650–60
Belonging to a Milanese family of painters, Giuseppe assisted his brother Carlo Francesco with frescoes
and altarpieces. He himself was better known for his portraits, in which he used richer colour.
Perhaps his palette — as well as the composition – of this self-portrait shows the influence of Titian.
(Pinacoteca di Brera, Milan, Italy)

ISAAC OLIVER (c. 1565–1617), c. 1590–95
Isaac Oliver was born in France. He came to England and trained as a miniature-artist with Nicholas Hilliard.
This self-portrait, in excellent condition, is typical of his work. Shading and light are used effectively,
and colours are vibrant. The work is painted on vellum mounted on card.
(Christie's Images, London, England)

BERNARD VAN ORLEY (c. 1488–1541), c. 1520
The Netherlandish artist worked in a northern European style that was strongly influenced by the ideals and practices
of the Italian Renaissance masters. The angle of the face to the picture plane in this painting was by
this period the standard one in portraiture and self-portraiture.
(Kunsthistorisches Museum, Vienna, Austria)

WILLIAM ORPEN (1878–1931), c. 1924
The Irish portrait-painter here depicted himself, palette in hand, in front of an infinity of self-portraits reflected in two mirrors. The vibrant style of this painting is characteristic of the artist, who worked quickly. Orpen had a large and fashionable practice and was one of the most successful portrait-painters working in Britain in the twentieth century.
(Fitzwilliam Museum, University of Cambridge, England)

PEDRO ORRENTE (1580–1645), c. 1630
The Spanish artist's sombre face is strongly lit and contrasts with his dark clothing. Most of his known paintings were religious works, either large canvases for altarpieces or small devotional pictures of Biblical scenes.
In 1633 he sought a position with the Holy Office of the Inquisition.
(Museo de Santa Cruz, Toledo, Spain)

GREGORIO PAGANI (1558–1605), c. 1592
For large-scale religious frescoes in churches of his native Florence, the Italian artist made many studies from life.
He was associated with a group of artists who wanted a new clarity of story-telling and naturalism in painting,
a directness found in his self-image as a painter of religious art.
(Galleria degli Uffizi, Florence, Italy)

SAMUEL PALMER (1805–81). C. 1824–25
The English Romantic painter drew this portrait of himself at about the age of twenty, in black chalk heightened with white on paper. The strong overhead light suggests that the drawing was done at night. It illustrates his rather clerical way of dressing, with a white cravat, a style that was old-fashioned for the time.
(Ashmolean Museum, Oxford, England)

PARMIGIANINO [FRANCESCO MAZZOLA] (1503–40), 1524
Painted on a curved panel measuring just over 15 inches (39 cm) in diameter, the artist painted his portrait as he saw
himself reflected in a barber's mirror; the convex glass exaggerated the size of his hand.
Exaggeration and distortion are both characteristics of Italian Mannerism.
(Kunsthistorisches Museum, Vienna, Austria)

SAMUEL JOHN PEPLOE (1871–1935), c. 1900
The piercing gaze and fluid brushwork of this self-portrait present an assured and cosmopolitan image
of the Scottish artist. Highly self-critical and a perfectionist, his concerns as an artist were focused on
the exploration of form in still-lifes and landscapes.
(Scottish National Gallery of Modern Art, Edinburgh, Scotland/Courtesy of Guy Peploe)

JEAN-BAPTISTE PERRONEAU (1715–83), C. 1747
The self-portrait is in oil on canvas, though Perroneau made a name for himself as a portraitist working in pastel.
His fine clothes and fearless look of self-appraisal promote this as the image of a gentleman rather than an artist.
(Musée des Beaux-Arts, Tours, France)

PABLO PICASSO (1881–1973), 1906
During a long and immensely creative life the Spanish painter, sculptor, printmaker and potter, who was active in
France, dominated European art and was the central model for modern perceptions of the contemporary artist.
This early self-likeness dates from the beginning of the breakdown of the Western tradition of illusionistic space.
(Philadelphia Museum of Art, USA/© Succession Picasso/DACS 1999)

PIERO DELLA FRANCESCA (c. 1415–92), after 1458
The Resurrection was painted by the Florentine on a wall of the Residenza in Borgo San Sepolcro in the artist's
characteristically robust style. According to tradition, Piero's self-portrait is included among the sleeping soldiers,
with his neck resting on the lid of the sarcophagus.
(Pinacoteca, Sansepolcro, Italy)

PINTURRICHIO [BERNARDINO DI BETTO] (1454–1513), 1502
The Umbrian painter's setting for the Annunciation, part of a fresco cycle for the Baglioni Chapel, is a magnificent
architectural interior, through which the eye is led to a distant landscape.
The artist's self-portrait is on the right-hand wall.
(Santa Maria Maggiore, Spello, Italy)

DETAIL
The framed self-portrait, inscribed tablet and, beneath, the detail of crossed paintbrushes serve as the artist's signature.
Beautifully painted still-life objects are displayed above.

CAMILLE PISSARRO (1830–1903), 1873
Born on St Thomas in the Dutch East Indies, Pissarro moved to Paris in 1855 and became a key figure in the
Impressionist circle. This self-portrait was painted the year before the first of the Impressionist exhibitions,
which were held between 1874 and 1886. Pissarro was the only artist to exhibit in all eight of them.
(Musée d'Orsay, Paris, France)

JACOPO DA PONTORMO (1494–1556), 1525–28.
This painted altarpiece in Santa Felicità, Florence, is known as the *Deposition* or *Lamentation*
and is the masterpiece of the Italian artist who decorated the Capponi Chapel.
It is painted in a typical Mannerist style, with exaggerated colours and figures in unnatural poses.
Pontormo includes himself as an observer on the right, represented in more neutral tones.
(Capponi Chapel, Santa Felicità, Florence, Italy)

Nicolas Poussin (1594–1665), 1650
The founder and master of French Classicism painted this self-portrait in Rome, where he spent most of his working life. The framed canvas in the background identifies him as a painter of allegorical subjects.
(Musée du Louvre, Paris, France)

GIULIO CESARE PROCACCINI (1574–1625), 1624
Procaccini was from a family of successful Italian artists and represents himself here proudly holding a gold medal on a chain, symbol of his achievements. In the background is a plaque or board bearing the painter's name.
The light falls upon the artist's face but all around is darkness, perhaps representing his fading career; the picture was painted a year before his death.
(Pinacoteca di Brera, Milan, Italy)

ARTHUR RACKHAM (1867–1939), 1907
This is 'The Mad Hatter's Tea Party' from Lewis Carroll's *Alice's Adventures in Wonderland* by the English illustrator.
Rackham was best known for his illustrations to classic children's stories and fairy-tales commissioned by the
publisher Heinemann between 1900 and 1914. The Mad Hatter in the drawing is a caricature of himself.
(British Library, London, England/© The Arthur Rackam pictures are reproduced with the kind
permission of his family)

HENRY RAEBURN (1756–1823), c. 1815
The picture was offered as a Diploma work on the Scottish painter's election to the Royal Academy, but it was turned
down as members' own portraits were inadmissable. Raeburn achieved great distinction as a portrait-painter.
In 1822 he was knighted by George IV and the following year appointed His Majesty's Limner for Scotland.
(National Gallery of Scotland, Edinburgh, Scotland)

RAPHAEL [RAFFAELLO SANZIO] (1483–1520), 1510–11
In his fresco of *The School of Athens* in the Stanza della
Segnatura of the Vatican, Raphael included a portrait of
himself as a witness to the discourses of the
philosophers of Antiquity. The painting is one of the
great secular works of the master from Urbino.
On the extreme right of the fresco, beside the painted
arch, Raphael depicted himself and a figure
believed to be Pinturicchio, a painter with whom he had
previously worked in Siena.
(Vatican Museums and Galleries, Vatican City, Italy)

RAPHAEL [RAFFAELLO SANZIO] (1483–1520), c.1519
The man with a sword in the foreground of Raphael's *Self-portrait with a Friend*,
while looking back at Raphael, points his finger out of the picture.
This and Raphael's gaze both seem to relate to a presence occupying the place of the onlooker.
(Musée du Louvre, Paris, France)

PAUL RAUD (1865–1930), 1900
The self-portrait by the Estonian artist, the left side of his face and hat outlined dramatically by light, was painted after
he had brought to an end a long series of commissioned portraits. Liberated from the restrictions imposed by such
work, Raud concentrated on more personal paintings such as this, freer in style and execution.
(Estonian Art Museum, Tallinnn, Estonia)

PAULA REGO (born 1935), 1993
The principal figure is not a likeness of the British artist, but the picture can be regarded as a self-portrait
by association entitled: *The Artist in her Studio*, it contains references to Rego's childhood in Portugal
and to her grandchildren. It is painted in acrylic on canvas.
(City Art Gallery, Leeds Museums and Galleries, England/Courtesy of Malborough Fine Art (London) Ltd)

REMBRANDT HARMENSZ. VAN RIJN (1606–69), 1629
In this panel painting the Dutch artist has depicted himself magnificently dressed in a mustard-coloured cloak
with a gold chain around his shoulders, and a plumed and jewelled beret. The costume has similarities
with dress of the previous century. This, of all his approximately forty painted self-portraits,
includes the most exquisite rendering of the texture of the various materials.
(Isabella Stewart Gardner Museum, Boston, USA)

REMBRANDT HARMENSZ. VAN RIJN (1606–69), 1630
The young Dutch artist's study of his own face, in a pen and ink drawing on paper, anticipates the series of etchings
he began soon afterwards. These illustrate his artistic interests and were investigations of a wide range of facial
expressions, using his own features as a model. They were intended to assist his rendition of character and emotion.
(Musée du Louvre, Paris, France)

REMBRANDT HARMENSZ. VAN RIJN (1606–69), 1631
The Dutch artist, newly arrived in Amsterdam from Leiden, and with a growing reputation as a portrait painter,
produced portraits of himself for established or potential patrons. In fancy Oriental costume and sword,
and with a spaniel, he presents a colourful and impressive account of himself and his abilities as a painter.
(Musée de la Ville de Paris, Musée du Petit-Palais, France)

Rembrandt Harmensz. Van Rijn (1606–69), 1633
In his velvet hat and coat, and with a gold chain, the Dutch artist's portrait of himself, signed with his first name in the
manner of the great Italian artists, portrays him as a man of substance and consequence. It was probably produced in
response to growing public recognition of his features and his artistic fame.
(Musée du Louvre, Paris, France)

The title of the painting, in oil on canvas, is *Self-portrait as the Prodigal Son in the Tavern*. The woman looking back over her shoulder has been identified as a likeness of Saskia. The subject of the picture is believed to be based on the Biblical parable of the prodigal son, with the painter and his wife serving as models for the figures.
(Staatliche Kunstsammlungen, Dresden, Germany)

REMBRANDT HARMENSZ. VAN RIJN (1606–69), 1660
Despite bankruptcy, and the loss of his lavish lifestyle and remarkable study collection of prints,
it would appear that the Dutch artist's fame as an artist still prompted public demand for his self-portraits.
(Musée du Louvre, Paris, France)

Rembrandt Harmensz. Van Rijn (1606–69), c. 1665–69
This direct and powerful self-portrait by Rembrandt is now one of the most popular images of the Dutch artist.
He is dressed in working clothes, with a white linen cap on his head and holding his palette, brushes and mahlstick.
He stands gazing out directly to the spectator, a pose that he altered on the canvas
from one in which he showed himself as an artist at work.
(Kenwood House, London, England)

Rembrandt Harmensz. Van Rijn (1606–69), 1669
This is one of three self-portraits of the great Dutch master painted in the last year of his life.
For over four decades he had painted, etched and drawn his own likeness to assist the development
of his art, and created self-images that promoted his considerable abilities and range of characterization.
(Mauritshuis, The Hague, The Netherlands)

GUIDO RENI (1575–1642), c. 1630
Despite his irascible nature, and the financial altercations that accompanied many of his commissions,
the Italian artist worked for the Borghese family and the Papal court in Rome, and the Gonzagas in Mantua.
He was regarded as the artistic heir of Raphael, and enjoyed fame in his own lifetime and in succeeding centuries.
(Galleria degli Uffizi, Florence, Italy)

PIERRE-AUGUSTE RENOIR (1841–1919), 1879
The artist's gaze, alert and full of purpose, is directed into the distance, which is rare in a self-portrait, and the head is seen from slightly below. The thick dabs of paint with which the French Impressionist indicated his own features are unlike his usual technique. The picture was exhibited at the second Impressionist exhibition in 1876.
(Clark Institute, Williamstown, USA)

PIERRE-AUGUSTE RENOIR (1841–1919), 1910
The painting is a touching self-image of the French Impressionist in old age, displaying a sense of uncertainty and
bewilderment at the change in his appearance brought about by time.
(Galerie Daniel Malingue, Paris, France)

ARCANGELO RESANI (1670–1740), c. 1713
This self-likeness is considered to be among the finest works of the Italian artist, who was much admired by
contemporaries for his rustic genre pieces and still-lifes. The woven straw basket,
as an object of craftsmanship, features in all his paintings.
(Galleria degli Uffizi, Florence, Italy)

JOSHUA REYNOLDS (1723–92), 1775
The English artist in this self-portrait wears the cap and gown of a Doctor of Civil Law from Oxford University;
the inscription on the scroll that he holds reads, 'Drawings by the Divine Michelangelo Bon . . .' In 1768 he was
appointed the first President of the Royal Academy of Arts and he was knighted the following year.
(Galleria degli Uffizi, Florence, Italy)

JOSHUA REYNOLDS (1723–92), c. 1780
Beside the painter is a bust of Michelangelo by Daniele da Volterra; Reynolds considered Michelangelo
the 'Homer of painting'. In the manner in which it is painted the self-portrait bears testimony
as well to Reynolds's admiration for Rembrandt.
(Royal Academy of Arts, London, England)

Joshua Reynolds (1723–92), 1792
The partially completed self-portrait is believed to have been on Reynolds's easel at the time of his death.
Towards the end of his life, before being overtaken by blindness, Reynolds delivered his Discourses at the Royal
Academy. In these he set out his doctrine on the Ideal in Art, achieved by recourse to 'reason and philosophy'.
(Chequers, Buckinghamshire, England)

Hᴀᴄɪɴᴛʜᴇ Rɪɢᴀᴜᴅ (1659–1743), 1716
The assurance of this self-portrait, painted full-face with the body slightly turned, reflects his position as the most
admired court painter to the French kings Louis XIV and Louis XV. The intention of portraiture at this period
was to display the sitter's rank rather than his individuality.
(Galleria degli Uffizi, Florence, Italy)

WILLIAM ROBINSON (1799–1839), c. 1835
Robinson was born in Leeds and trained under the foremost portrait painter of the period, Thomas Lawrence.
This image shows Robinson in a formal pose similar to the ones he used for other subjects
such as his portraits of the young Disraeli and Thomas Philip, Earl de Grey.
(City Art Gallery, Leeds Museums and Galleries, England)

NORMAN ROCKWELL (1894–1978), 1925
From 1916 to 1963 the American artist produced the cover illustrations for *The Saturday Evening Post*.
This self-portrait, the original design for the 18 April 1925 edition of the magazine, is part realistic,
part sentimental in the manner characteristic of Rockwell's illustrations.
(Christie's Images, London, England)

Ritratto di Giulio Romano.

13328

GIULIO ROMANO (1499–1546), c. 1535
The Italian artist executed this self-portrait in pastel, which creates a soft and subtle impression.
The pastel was made from ground white chalk and powder colour. First used in the fifteenth century,
its production was more advanced, and it was more widely used, in the eighteenth century.
(Gabinetto dei Disegni e Stampe, Uffizi, Florence, Italy)

SALVATOR ROSA (1615–73), c. 1641
From an affluent and educated background, the colourful and original Italian artist used learned allusions in this,
his earliest known self-portrait as *Silence*. The moody background and his melancholic, taciturn expression
describe a sensibility that made his work, particularly his rugged mountainous landscapes,
popular among English collectors in the following century.
(National Gallery, London, England)

SALVATOR ROSA (1615–73), c. 1650–60
Rosa was particularly interested in capturing the nuances of characterization and often used himself as a model
in studies of pose and expression. Although his figures were sometimes stiff, the dark tones and dramatic
shadows create an expressive and sombre mood of religious exaltation and awe.
(Hermitage, St Petersburg, Russia)

DANTE GABRIEL ROSSETTI (1828–82), 1861
The self-portrait, a simple, intense study of the head of the Pre-Raphaelite, is in pencil on paper.
Rossetti, an English artist of Italian descent, had eschewed formal art training
and was sometimes criticized for his variable skills as a draughtsman.
(Birmingham Museums and Art Gallery, England)

ALESSANDRO ROSI (1627–1707), c. 1650
A painter of religious subjects for churches and historical compositions for private collectors in his native Florence, this Italian painter has created a dramatic and stark self-image. The black felt hat is tipped back to show moody and aloof features, brought into focus with dramatic lighting.
(Galleria degli Uffizi, Florence, Italy)

HENRI ROUSSEAU (1844–1910), 1890
The French naïve painter was a 'Sunday' painter, known as 'Le Douanier Rousseau' because his everyday job was as a
petty Customs official. Here, in the painting entitled *Myself: Portrait-Landscape*, he portrays himself as the
quintessential French artist, complete with beret, palette and brush; he stands in front of the Seine,
with the Eiffel Tower in the background and a balloon in the sky.
(Národní Galerie, Prague, Czech Republic)

HENRI ROUSSEAU (1844–1910), c. 1900–3
Self-portrait with an Oil Lamp shows the painter as a man of distinction, with smooth hair and carefully brushed-up moustache. He painted a portrait of his wife with the same oil lamp as a pair to this. Although acknowledging his technical limitations, he described himself in 1895 as being 'in the process of becoming one of our great realist painters'.
(Musée Picasso, Paris, France)

HENRI ROUSSEAU (1844–1910), 1908
The picture is a group portrait of Rousseau's
neighbour's family. The greengrocer had just bought a
dapple grey pony, and he and his wife and children are
seated in the cart. A photograph was taken of them,
including the dog, and the horse and cart, and the
painting was based on this. The man on the right
wearing a straw hat, who was not in the photograph,
is Rousseau himself.
(Musée de l'Orangerie, Paris, France)

PETER PAUL RUBENS (1577–1640), c. 1602
Presided over by a bust of the Roman philosopher Seneca, the Flemish artist declares his own classical learning,
but affirms his artistic role as observer and recorder by detaching himself from the group that includes his brother
Philip, the humanist scholar Justus Lipsius and another pupil, Johannes Woverius.
(Galleria Palatina, Florence, Italy)

DETAIL
Despite his artistic success in Italy, where this picture was painted, Rubens returned to the southern Netherlands, where he maintained an aristocratic lifestyle and was given another role as a diplomat. Painting at the great European courts, he produced magnificent cycles of allegorical paintings glorifying his princely patrons.

PETER PAUL RUBENS (1577–1640), c. 1609
The Flemish artist has pictured himself with his first wife, Isabella Brandt, in a traditional north European matrimonial double portrait. The idea of love in the union is allegorically stated in the setting of a honeysuckle bower and the unity of the poses; Rubens's role as master and protector is indicated by his higher position.
(Alte Pinakothek, Munich, Germany)

PETER PAUL RUBENS (1577–1640), 1623–5
The painting was acquired by Cosimo III de' Medici and added to the collection of self-portraits
formed by his uncle, Cardinal Leopoldo de' Medici, hung in the Palazzo Pitti. Cosimo established the collection
in the Uffizi, in the Galleria degli autoritratti.
(Galleria degli Uffizi, Florence, Italy)

PETER PAUL RUBENS (1577–1640), c. 1625–30.
The informal character and neutral background of this self-likeness of the Flemish artist suggests that it may
have been a prototype for use in more finished and detailed portrait compositions. It was also engraved,
as an image for circulation of one of the most versatile and influential artists of northern Europe.
(Christie's Images, London, England)

VENTURA DI ARCANGELO SALIMBENI (1568–1613), c. 1610
The dashing self-image with a pistol is of an Italian painter who in his youth worked in Rome on the decoration of the
Vatican Library. Returning to his native Siena, where he was considered a leading personality,
he painted religious and mythological frescoes there and in Lucca and Perugia.
(Galleria degli Uffizi, Florence, Italy)

JOHN SINGER SARGENT (1856–1925), 1906
This is a likeness of the American-born artist at the age of fifty, in which he gives away very little about himself.
He painted it in Italy, for the Uffizi collection of self-portraits;
to be invited to contribute to this famous collection was a great honour.
(Galleria degli Uffizi, Florence, Italy)

ANDREA DEL SARTO (1486–1531), 1528–30
The self-image by the Florentine High Renaissance painter is a masterpiece of gentle thoughtfulness.
It was painted in the unusual materials of tempera on tile. Del Sarto was known as *Andrea senza errori*,
Andrea the faultless, due to his sureness of execution.
(Galleria degli Uffizi, Florence, Italy)

GODFRIED SCHALCKEN (1643–1706), c. 1677
The Dutch artist specialized in depicting the effects of light on figures and objects, illuminating
part of the composition and releasing the rest into shadow. The self-portrait follows the favoured theme
of a face partially caught in the light from a candle, resulting in a remarkable feeling of intimacy.
(Leamington Spa Museum and Art Gallery, England)

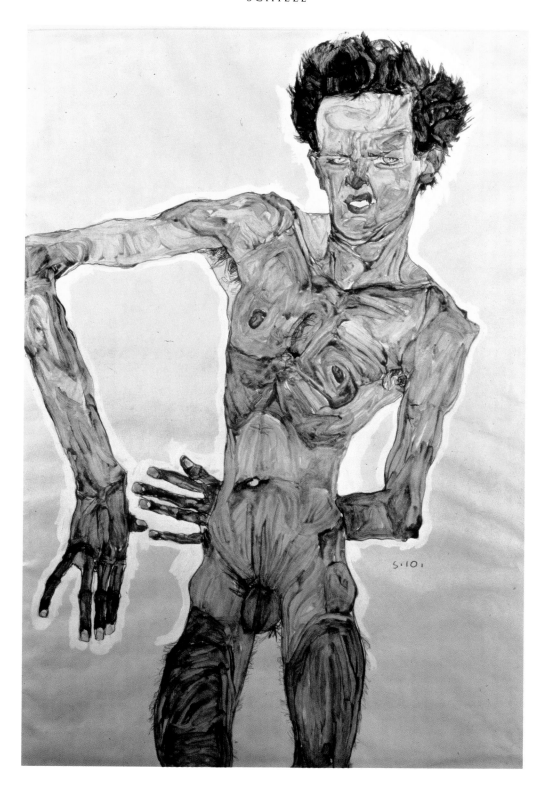

EGON SCHIELE (1890–1918, 1910
The nude self-portrait by the Viennese Expressionist is full of *Angst*. The gestures are contorted, the facial expression
an agonized grimace and the body an unhealthy grey, knobbly and sprouting coarse hair.
It is executed in pencil, watercolour, glue and bodycolour.
(Graphische Sammlung Albertina, Vienna, Austria)

EGON SCHIELE (1890–1918), 1910
This self-portrait is of the same year, worked in pencil, watercolour and glue, with the body outlined in gouache.
The element of grotesque self-disgust is again pronounced, the oblique angle of the artist's
emaciated body contributing to the impression of anguish.
(Graphische Sammlung Albertina, Vienna, Austria)

ZINAIDA EVGENIEVNA SEREBRYAKOVA (1884–1967), 1909

Entitled *Self-portrait at the Dressing-table*, this work by the Russian painter was included in the seventh Union of Russian Artists exhibition in Moscow and St Petersburg. The composition and scumbled technique, with an opaque layer of paint laid over another of a different colour, shows an awareness of the Old Masters. (Tretyakov Gallery, Moscow, Russia/© ADAGP, Paris and DACS, London 1999)

GINO SEVERINI (1883–1966), 1913
The fragmented, hard-lined style of the self-portrait by the Italian demonstrates his commitment to Futurism,
a movement of which he was one of the principal exponents. The painting is a multi-faceted view of the artist
in spectacles and hat, and with a cigarettte, painted the year he held a one-man exhibition in London.
(Private Collection/© ADAGP, Paris and DACS, London 1999)

Fedor Mikhailovich Slavyansky (1819–76), 1857
The Russian artist, palette in hand, stands with his family, in costume and surroundings that are European in style.
The profusion of plants, the striped awning and the Turkey carpet of the balcony all demonstrate the fashionable
nineteenth-century preoccupation with merging the garden with the house.
(State Russian Museum, St Petersburg, Russia)

GERARD TERBORCH (1617–81), C. 1668
The Dutch artist was known for his naturalistic genre paintings, and miniature and full-length portraits.
As with his own image, his portraits at this time focused less on the individual status and trappings previously seen
and more on individuality, and the virtues of honesty and sobriety.
(Bode-Museum, Berlin, Germany)

WILLIAM MAKEPEACE THACKERAY (1811–63), c. 1848
Following the success of *Vanity Fair* the English novelist bought himself a horse, a black cob, as a symbol
of his prosperity. When he was a young man Thackeray had studied drawing in Paris
and contributed satirical illustrations as well as articles to such magazines as *Punch*.
The drawing of himself belonged to his close confidante Mrs Brookfield.
(*Scribner's Magazine*, 1887)

JACOPO ROBUSTI TINTORETTO (1519–94), c. 1546–8
Although he practised as an independent master from 1539, the young Italian artist struggled for recognition.
This simple self-likeness, of great intensity, was painted about the time he received his first important public
commission in his native Venice, for the decorations of the Scuola Grande di San Marco.
(Philadelphia Museum of Art, USA)

JACOPO ROBUSTI TINTORETTO (1519–94), 1588
The most prolific Venetian master of his time had a long and busy career executing prestigious public commissions,
including the decoration of the Ducal Palace. However, his work was criticised for its swift, abbreviated style
and lack of finish, and his employment of numerous assistants.
(Musée du Louvre, Paris, France)

JAMES JACQUES JOSEPH TISSOT (1836–1902), c. 1865
Edmond de Goncourt described Tissot in 1890 as 'this complex being, a blend of mysticism and phoneyness,
laboriously intelligent in spite of an unintelligent skull and the eyes of a boiled fish, passionate,
finding every two or three years a new passion with which he contracts a little new lease on life.'
(Fine Arts Museums of San Francisco, USA)

TITIAN [TIZIANO VECELLIO] (c. 1488–1576), c. 1512
Titian's *Portrait of a Man* is said to be a portrait of the artist himself. His prominent right arm resting on a ledge in the foreground is the model for many later portraits, in Venice and elsewhere; in the seventeenth century the painting, then wrongly thought to be a portrait of Lodovico Ariosto, the Italian poet, was in Amsterdam.
(National Gallery, London, England)

TITIAN [TIZIANO VECELLIO] (c. 1488–1576), c. 1768
In this picture Titian portrayed himself as the revered elderly painter that he was, his work as powerful as ever before.
Dressed in dark clothing, against a dark backdrop, his face in profile and the hand holding a paintbrush are strongly lit.
(Prado, Madrid, Spain)

HENRI DE TOULOUSE-LAUTREC (1864–1901), C. 1882–83
The self-portrait was painted soon after Lautrec arrived in Paris, where he began by attending Léon Bonnat's studio.
He was looking at himself in a mirror with the objects on the mantelpiece in front of him in the reflected image.
(Musée Toulouse-Lautrec, Albi, France)

HENRI DE TOULOUSE-LAUTREC (1864–1901), C. 1885
During his lifetime Lautrec was known primarily as a poster-designer. He was an assured and expressive draughtsman,
a caricaturist of himself and his contemporaries, and is now best remembered as a painter of Parisian low life.
(Musée Toulouse-Lautrec, Albi, France)

HENRI DE TOULOUSE-LAUTREC (1864–1901), 1896
As a boy Lautrec fractured both legs in a riding accident, which affected his physical development.
In this lithograph he makes fun of his own appearance – a fully-developed torso on short legs –
which made him the object of public curiosity.
(Musée Toulouse-Lautrec, Albi, France)

MAURICE QUENTIN DE LA TOUR (1704–88), C. 1739
The amiable face of the French artist as portrayed by himself demonstrates his mastery of his chosen medium.
He never worked in oils and was one of the most celebrated pastellists of the eighteenth century. The
naturalness of his style is especially evident in his self-portraits and in portraits of his friends.
(Sotheby's, London, England)

JEAN FRANÇOIS DE TROY (1679–1752), 1696
The French painter specialized in portraying contemporary manners, fashions and pastimes for the Parisian élite.
Commissions were also received from Louis XV for decorative painting at Versailles,
and as a successful and rich artist he became the Director of the French Academy in Rome.
(Galleria degli Uffizi, Florence, Italy)

LAURITS REGNER TUXEN (1853–1927), c. 1920
A society portrait painter in Denmark, Russia and England, the Danish painter worked steadily from the 1880s
until 1914 for the courts of three English monarchs. This self-portrait, like the portraits he did of his own family
in the last decade of his life, is less formal, less finished, than his earlier work.
(Bonhams, London, England)

MARY FRASER TYTLER (1849–1938), 1882
The little-known English artist portrays herself in this watercolour with quiet subtlety.
The restricted range of tones emphasizes the mood of introspection created by the expression on her face.
(Trustees of the Watts Gallery, Compton, England)

LEON UNDERWOOD (1890–75), 1921
This is a youthful self-likeness, an etching, by this original, individual and undervalued British artist, who restlessly
explored many art forms. Having trained in etching and engraving, he went on to become a powerful sculptor and
painter, whose imaginative representation of the human form investigated afresh the Classical tradition in Western art.
(Wolseley Fine Arts, London, England/Courtesy of Garth Underwood)

FÉLIX VALLOTTON (1865–1925), 1891
This Swiss-born printmaker and art critic was based in Paris, where he learned to excel in the medium of woodcut,
at that time enjoying an international revival of interest influenced by the popularity of Japanese art.
This decorative self-likeness is a woodcut on textured cream wove paper.
(Wolseley Fine Arts, London, England)

GIORGIO VASARI (1511–74), 1567

Vasari was the author of *Lives of the Most Excellent Painters, Sculptors and Architects*, first published in 1550.
On this is based much of the knowledge about the art and artists of Renaissance Italy. Vasari was a painter
as well as a biographer, and the portrait was by Vasari himself or by an artist belonging to his circle.
(Galleria degli Uffizi, Florence, Italy)

DIEGO RODRIGUEZ DE SILVA Y VELÁZQUEZ (1599–1660), c. 1657
One of the most important European artists of the seventeenth century, the Spaniard portrays himself in traditional head and shoulders length against a dark background. Velázquez was invested with the Cross of Santiago in 1659, and portraits of him after that date include the badge of that order.
(Galleria degli Uffizi, Florence, Italy)

DIEGO RODRIGUEZ DE SILVA Y VELÁZQUEZ (1599–1660), 1656
This picture, known as *Las Meniñas*, is considered to be the Spanish painter's masterpiece. The canvas depicts the infanta Margarita surrounded by her maids of honour (*meniñas*), her servants, dwarfs and clowns, in a room in the Alcázar. To the left the painter has included a portrait of himself. The mirror at the back of the room reflects an image of Philip IV and his queen, who are thus both the models for the canvas Velázquez is working on and the viewers of the scene.
(Prado, Madrid, Spain)

DETAIL
Velázquez is depicted brush in hand, standing back from his enormous canvas,
studying or else surprised by the king and queen.
(Prado, Madrid, Spain)

CONSTANTYN VERHOUT [VOORHOUT] (fl. 1663–67)
Little is known about this Dutch artist, but the picture *The Painter and his Pupil* has survived, taking the theme of a lesson. Verhout portrays himself as the artist absorbed in an anatomical drawing, while a young apprentice watches admiringly. Mortality and the transferral of knowledge between generations are themes that are touched upon.
(Musée des Beaux-Arts, Caen, France)

EMILE JEAN HORACE VERNET (1789–1863), 1835
Vernet was Director of the French Academy in Rome from 1828 to 1834 and visited Algeria several times between
1833 and 1853. He depicts himself here in his studio, attired in and surrounded by the Arabian props he collected
for use in his paintings. The artist leans against a stove which kept the studio and his models warm.
(Hermitage, St Petersburg, Russia)

PAOLO CALIARI VERONESE (1528–88), 1562–63
This monumental oil painting of *The Marriage Feast at Cana* was commissioned for the refectory of the monastery of San Giorgio Maggiore in Venice.
The Italian artist has included a self-image as a viol player. Obliged to work without the assistance of pupils, it took Veronese fifteen months to complete.
(Musée du Louvre, Paris, France)

MARIE-LOUISE-ELIZABETH VIGÉE-LEBRUN (1755–1842), 1786
The French portrait-painter here represents herself as a model of feminity and maternal devotion.
The painting contains all the elements of her extremely popular style: informality,
animated facial expression and the careful observation of the fall of cloth.
(Musée du Louvre, Paris, France)

MARIE-LOUISE-ELIZABETH VIGÉE-LEBRUN (1755–1842), 1789
In the year that Madame Vigée-Lebrun painted this self-portrait she fled the country with the daughter she clasps to her: Marie-Antoinette's patronage of her was causing comment damaging to her reputation. Similar in subject-matter to the previous painting, and only a few years later in date, it shows the influence of Neoclassism.
(Musée du Louvre, Paris, France)

MARIE-LOUISE-ELIZABETH VIGÉE-LEBRUN (1755–1842), 1790.
The self-portrait was painted for the Uffizi collection during the time the artist was in Italy escaping from the Revolution in France. She herself made copies of the pictures she painted of herself, and this one, particularly has been much copied by other artists.
(Galleria degli Uffizi, Florence, Italy)

GIUSEPPE PELIZZA DA VOLPEDO (1868–1907), 1899
The Italian's portrait of himself has a powerful emotional presence. The strong verticality of the composition
accentuates the sense of detachment that seems to be suggested by his pose and the expression on his face.
(Galleria degli Uffizi, Florence, Italy)

SIMON VOUET (1590–1649), 1620
Vouet was a prolific French artist who turned his hand to mythological, religious and portrait painting. This is characteristic of his rather theatrical style and shows the artist, with mouth slightly open, against a plain background. Formerly thought to be by Caravaggio, the picture was painted while Vouet was in Italy.
(Musée des Beaux-Arts, Arles, France)

FERDINAND GEORG WALDMÜLLER (1793–1865), 1828
The Austrian artist was famous for his portraits emphasizing elegance and refinement.
This self-portrait conveys both those qualities, with the artist taking a confident frontal pose.
Waldmüller was also an important landscape painter from the 1830s, and chooses a natural background here.
The paeony in the foreground is a symbol of beauty and accomplishment.
(Österreichische Galerie, Vienna, Austria)

Cecile Walton (1891–1956), 1920
The Scottish artist's painting on the subject of
motherhood is entitled *Romance*. Walton herself,
as the mother, holds up the newborn baby and gazes at it
in solemn adoration and wonderment. The other child
looks on with equal seriousness. The still-life details
in the composition add to the sense of tranquillity.
(Scottish National Portrait Gallery, Edinburgh, Scotland)

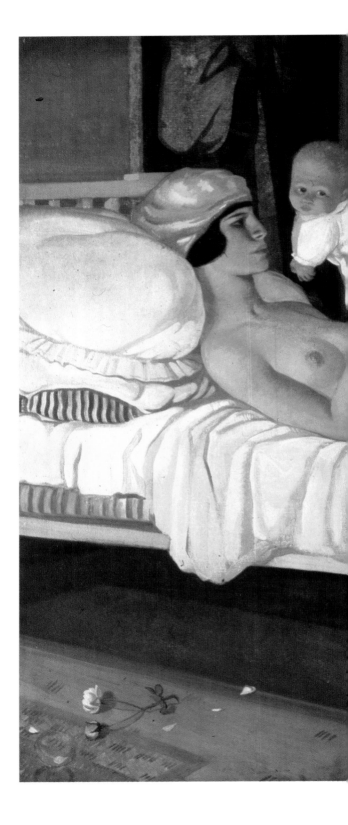

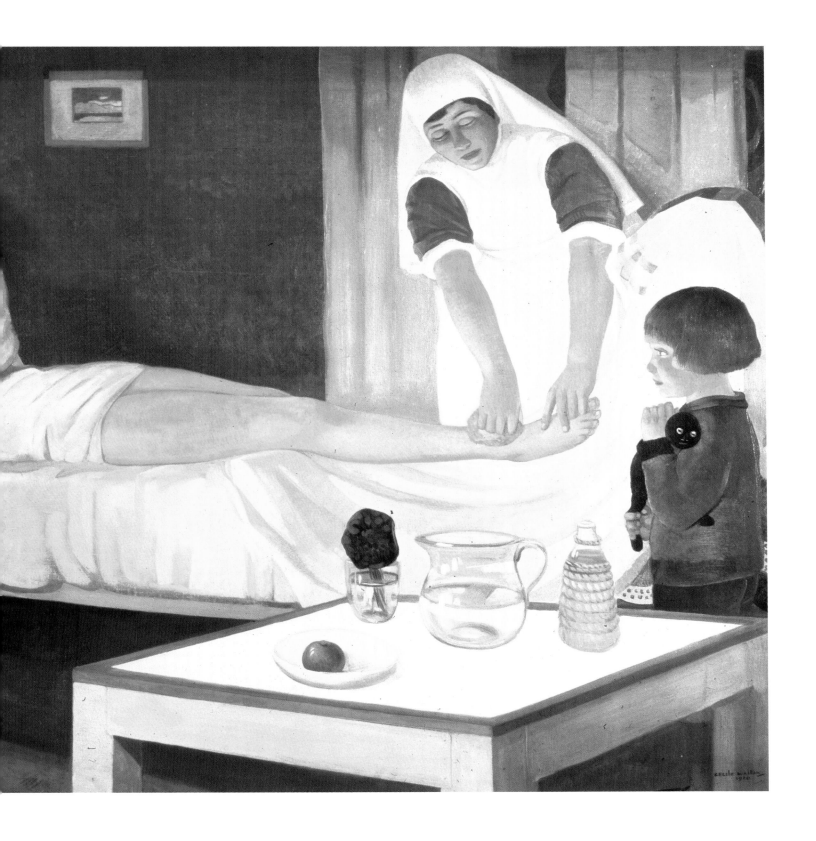

ANDY WARHOL (1930–87), 1967
Advised to feed his celebrity with self-images, the American began a sequence of self-portraits in the early 1960s,
just after his sensational emergence as a Pop artist. Through the primary use of acrylic and silk-screen ink on canvas in
different colourways, and in multiple series, the image celebrates mass consumption through reproduction.
(Private Collection)

GEORGE FREDERICK WATTS (1817–1904), 1834
The sketchily-done portrait of the English artist dates from when he was seventeen and a year before he was admitted
to the Royal Academy Schools. He was later to write, 'I paint myself constantly, that is to say whenever I want to make
an experiment in method or colour and I am not in the humour to make a design.'
(Trustees of the Watts Gallery, Compton, England)

GEORGE FREDERICK WATTS (1817–1904), 1879
Watts painted this sombre self-portrait for an exhibition at the Uffizi. It has been suggested that the Englishman
was attempting to make himself resemble Titian in old age. One of the most successful portrait-painters
of the late Victorian perid, Ruskin called him a genius.
(Trustees of the Watts Gallery, Compton, England)

JOSEPH WERNER (1637–1710), 1662
The ingeniously composed miniature by the Swiss artist was painted by him at the age of twenty-five
and is the only known work of his from that period. He here exhibits the extreme technical prowess
of a painter trained in the academic tradition.
(Victoria & Albert Museum, London, England)

JAMES ABBOTT McNEILL WHISTLER (1834–1903), 1865–66
The American-born artist was living in London when he painted this sketch of himself in his studio.
Executed in oils on paper, it was done in preparation for a larger picture that was never completed.
The style of the sketch is strongly influenced by Japanese art.
(Art Institute of Chicago, USA)

JAMES ABBOTT MCNEILL WHISTLER (1834–1903), c. 1872
The self-image of the artist is entitled *Arrangement in Grey*. Whistler described painting as the 'poetry of sight' and
believed that subject-matter was not relevant in the creation of colour harmonies.
A wit and a dandy, he looks out of the portrait with cool detachment.
(The Detroit Institute of Arts, USA, Gift of Henry Glover Stevens)

BENJAMIN WILLIAMS (1831–1923), c. 1915
In this self-portrait the British painter is presented as an everyday working man, in typical early twentieth-century attire. Williams's easel is closed up, his palette put aside and he turns his back on his work, making no reference to it.
(Birmingham Museums and Art Gallery, England)

I. J. WILLIS (Nineteenth century), c. 1820–30
This self-portrait by a talented English amateur watercolourist depicts the artist at work. The young lady sits at her desk with her watercolour box, palette, and a vase of flowers in front of her. The room is naturally lit and furnished in typical Regency style. Behind the artist, under a side-table, can be seen her portfolio.
(Rafael Valls Gallery, London, England)

WINCENTY WODZINOWSKY (1864–1940), 1905
Wodzinowsky trained at the School of Fine Arts in
Cracow and was one of several Polish artists of the
period who emphasized patriotism in their work.
Here, the seemingly troubled artist is supported by
a woman, perhaps representing Poland, against the
stormy background of a native landscape.
(Mazovian Museum, Plock, Poland)

JOSEPH WRIGHT OF DERBY (1734–97), C. 1773–74
This self-portrait, with penetrating and detached gaze, is of an important English artist who never left his native Derby.
Having completed his first artistic training, he pictures himself in Van Dyck dress,
stating his youthful attachment to the historic tradition of English portraiture.
(Private Collection)

FELIKS MICHAL WYGRZYWALSKI (1875–1944), 1910
This striking self-portrait of the Polish painter makes no attempt to portray the role of the artist.
It is a thoroughly personal image in which the painter uses his own face as the model,
and explores light, shadow and colour. It is executed in pastel and distemper on paper.
(Mazovian Museum, Plock, Poland)

Stanislaw Wyspianski (1869–1907), 1902
In the Polish artist's portrait of himself he submits his face to intense scrutiny. The head is set against a background of stylized flowers with a distinctly Art Nouveau flavour. The work, one of a series of self-portraits, is executed in pastel on paper. Wyspianski is best known as a designer of the applied arts, and especially stained glass.
(Narodowe Muzeum, Warsaw, Poland)

JOHANN ZOFFANY (1733–1810), 1756
This artistic display of youthful virtuosity by the German-born artist may have been done while Zoffany was studying
in Rome. In 1760 he arrived in London, where he found great success as a painter of theatre scenes and informal
portrait groups, or conversation pieces, for patrons that included the royal family.
(National Gallery of Victoria, Melbourne, Australia, purchased through the Art Foundation of Victoria)

RECOMMENDED READING
Borzello, Frances: *Seeing Ourselves: Women's Self-portraits*; London, 1998.
Brilliant, Richard: *Portraiture*; London 1991.
Gasser, Manuel: *Self-portraits: From the Fifteenth Century to the Present Day*; London 1963.
Gregori, Mina: *Paintings in the Uffizi and Pitti Galleries*; Boston, 1994.
Kelly, Sean and Lucie-Smith, Edward: *The Self Portrait, A Modern View*; London, 1987.
Kenneir, Joan (ed.): *The Artist by Himself: Self-portrait Drawings from Youth to Old Age*; London, 1980.
McQuillan, Melissa: *Impressionist Portraits*; London, 1986.
Woods-Marsden, Joanna: *Renaissance Self-portraiture: The Visual Construction of Identity and the Social Status of the Artist*; London, 1998.

INDEX OF ARTISTS